DISPERSING POWER
SOCIAL MOVEMENTS AS ANTI-STATE FORCES

DISPERSING POWER
SOCIAL MOVEMENTS AS ANTI-STATE FORCES

By Raúl Zibechi

Translated by Ramor Ryan

Forewords by Ben Dangl and John Holloway

AK
PRESS
EDINBURGH · OAKLAND · BALTIMORE

Dispersing Power: Social Movements as Anti-State Forces

ISBN-13: 978-1-84935-011-2

Library of Congress Control Number: 2010925753

AK Press   AK Press
674-A 23rd Street   PO Box 12766
Oakland, CA 94612   Edinburgh, EH8 9YE
USA   Scotland
www.akpress.org   www.akuk.com
akpress@akpress.org   ak@akedin.demon.co.uk

The above addresses would be delighted to provide you with the latest AK
Press distribution catalog, which features the several thousand books, pam-
phlets, zines, audio and video products, and stylish apparel published and/
or distributed by AK Press. Alternatively, visit our web site for the complete
catalog, latest news, and secure ordering.

Visit us at www.akpress.org *and* www.revolutionbythebook.akpress.org.

Printed in Canada on acid-free paper with union labor.
Interior design by JR
Indexed by Chris Dodge
Cover design by Chris Wright (seldomwright.com)

Table of Contents

Translator's note

by *Ramor Ryan*

It must be a rare occurrence when translating becomes an actual lived-experience, as the words and text on the page begin to reflect and come alive in the surrounding world. So it was in the winter of 2009, as I began to work on the translation of this book. I awoke one morning in my home in San Cristobal de las Casas, Chiapas, Mexico to the industrious sounds of two hundred indigenous families from the countryside invading and occupying an unused parcel of land adjoining our house. They set about constructing basic dwellings, pirating electricity, digging wells, and organizing the space collectively. They were not Zapatistas, but hung banners proclaiming Tierra y Libertad (Land and Freedom), and demanded indigenous rights. Was that the morning I began working on the chapter "The Self-Constructed City"?

The state sent in the riot police a few weeks later, just as I had moved onto the next chapter, "Everyday Life and Insurrection." The squatters fought back with sticks and stones, defending their small community with all the passion of rebel insurrectionists. And they won. In an interesting parallel to the Indians of El Alto, they spurned leaders, publicly denouncing those who attempted to speak on their behalf. They dispersed power and refused to allow a separate body of leaders to emerge. Or, as Zibechi writes of the El Alto uprising, "the community continues to function as a dispersal machine, always avoiding the concentration of power, and by allowing everyone to be a leader or commander, it inhibits the emergence of leaders with power over the long-term."

Translating *Dispersing Power* thus became a sociological, anthropological, and political lesson in the reality around me on the outskirts of San Cristobal. Clearly, Zibechi's important book is relevant not only to El Alto and Bolivia, but also to Mexico and much of the continent. This influenced my translation of the work: I attempt to use an everyday language that will be familiar to engaged, English-speaking readers and will hopefully resonate with them, in their own context and place.

This translation is the fruit of what must be properly described as a collective effort. A number of friends and compañeros have contributed their time and effort. Esteban Véliz Madina and Angelo Moreno were responsible for deciphering the Epilogue by Situaciones Colectivos and worked diligently to make it readable. In Favela—rebel territory within San Cristobal—inhabitants and visitors offered their two cents: I thank Esteban, Cui, Izas, Lord Red Eirigi, and Orlando. Further afield, Luigi Carlos Celentano, Brenda del Rocio Aguilar Marroquin, Michael McCaughan, Ben Dangl, and April Howard offered indispensable insights and commentary. AK Press is a radical and quintessential publishing house. It has been a seamless pleasure working with Zach Blue and Charles Weigl. I am grateful to my long-standing friend Chuck Morse for his discipline and professionalism in proofreading. His rigorous appraisal of the manuscript is, I hope, apparent in the final translation. Nevertheless, I take full responsibility for any errors or inaccuracies that have occurred in the translation, despite this proper flotilla of good counsel.

Finally, I wish to thank he who has accompanied me throughout the whole process, going without my undivided attention to facilitate the work: my young son, Ixim.

Foreword to the English Edition

by Benjamin Dangl

Bolivia is located in the heart of South America and is a country of majestic beauty, with enormous mountain ranges, dry plains, rolling farmland and expansive jungles. It is an exceptionally politicized place; countless workers and students are active in radical unions and organizations, roadblocks and strikes are regular occurrences across the country, and nearly non-stop protests fill the streets of its capital city, La Paz.

The country is currently going through profound social, cultural, and political changes. Though around sixty percent of its population self-identify as indigenous, just over fifty years ago, members of this indigenous majority were not even allowed in the plaza in front of the presidential palace. Now, that same palace is occupied by Evo Morales, an indigenous, former coca grower and union organizer who began his first term in 2006 after a tremendous victory at the polls. Since coming to power, the Morales administration has partially nationalized gas reserves, convened an assembly to rewrite the country's constitution, distributed unused land to farmers, and granted long overdue rights to indigenous people.

Leading up to the rocky and hopeful period of the Morales administration was a series of uprisings against neoliberalism and state repression, the most dramatic and far-reaching being the Gas War of 2003, in which people across the country rose up against a plan to export Bolivian gas to the US for a low price. Many also protested the unpopular policies and tactics of the Gonzalo Sánchez de Lozada government.

El Alto, a rapidly-growing city outside of La Paz, was in the vanguard of this national movement. Residents of the city organized massive road blockades, street barricades and marches that shut the roads down, pressuring those in La Paz to listen to their demands for the renunciation of Sánchez de Lozada and an end to the exploitative gas exportation plan. The courageous people of El Alto were victorious in ousting the president and pressuring the government to change its gas policies. In many ways, Morales's election owes a lot to the space and momentum created by El Alto. Morales's time in office has not been without contradictions and challenges, and his relationship with the social movements that helped pave the way to his election has had its ups and downs.

On May 1 of 2006, Morales announced the partial national-ization of Bolivia's gas reserves. Raúl Zibechi wrote in *La Jornada* of the president's actions and the legacy of El Alto: "It was during those days [in October 2003] that hydrocarbons were nationalized, because the decree Evo Morales signed on May 1st did not do any-thing more than legally sanction something that had been won in the streets." He continued, "The insurrectionary moment passed to the institutional moment."

Bolivia was not the only country in the region to pass from an "insurrectionary moment" to an "institutional movement." With self-described left-leaning governments in power in Ecuador, Argentina, Venezuela, Brazil, Paraguay, and Uruguay—that were ushered into office thanks in part to the popular movements in their country—the relationship between the insurrection and the institution is perhaps now more complex and crucial than it has been for decades.

Ecuador offers an example of this relationship. Throughout years of grassroots campaigns, protests, and direct action, the indige-nous movements in Ecuador pushed for a participatory, constitution-al assembly and against the destruction of the Amazon by neoliberal government policies and oil companies. Presidential candidate Rafa-el Correa then rode that wave of discontent and popular energy into the presidential palace in 2006, only to turn on the same movements that were essential to his election. While bringing about notable pro-gressive changes, he also began criminalizing the indigenous move-ment's protest tactics, pushing them out of the transformative politi-cal space they had created, and centralizing his own power. Similar stories have played out between governments and movements across the region.

Zibechi navigated this sociopolitical terrain in a February 2009 article for the Americas Program. He wrote that in varying degrees, this regional electoral shift to the left has meant "the marginaliza-tion of the social movements, which in the 1990s and at the start of 2000 were the main players in resistance to the neoliberal model; the dominant contradiction has been the dynamic between the gov-ernment and the right, an issue that pushed many social movements into a pro-state position that has appeared largely avoidable; some tendencies aim to move the social movements toward new bases of support, employing new causes and forms of intervention." Signifi-cantly however, he writes that in Bolivia "movements have not been defeated and continue to maintain an important capacity to mobilize their bases of support and pressure both the government and the rightwing."

Dispersing Power offers an exciting account of why social movements in Bolivia are so resilient and powerful, making the publication of this book timely; it focuses on the most vibrant social movements that preceded the election of one of the most dynamic and intriguing presidents among the region's new left.

So much of what Bolivians have organized against, particularly schools of economic thought, originated in the US. Readers in the US need to understand not only how these elements of imperialism work, but also what people in countries like Bolivia are working toward as alternatives to neoliberalism. It is that building of a better world that is dealt with in this book; many lessons and helpful strategies for activists around the world can be found in these pages.

The centuries-old debates surrounding indigenous power, community and the re-founding of Bolivia to reflect its indigenous culture were rekindled after the passage of Bolivia's new constitution in January of 2009. The changes in this constitution, along with much of the rhetoric and policies of the Morales administration, focus in part on empowering indigenous forms of decision making, governance, community justice, and social relations. *Dispersing Power* examines this ongoing process of "decolonization" by drawing from what indigenous societies and thinkers have been living, proposing, and working toward for centuries.

El Alto is currently far from a utopia; poverty, corruption, exploitation—the common challenges that plague many urban areas—are widespread in this city. But El Alto's legacy of revolt lives on. The Gas War of 2003 was a transformative period partly because it drew from a history of indigenous and popular revolts. This book is an invaluable resource on a rebellion that deserves to be read about and researched extensively. *Dispersing Power* examines not only the roots of this uprising, but also the solidarity, collaboration, support networks, tactics, and strategies that were used by the people of El Alto, and others, to make their revolutionary work successful not only during the Gas War, but in everyday life.

In this sense, *Dispersing Power* is a wonderful example of Zibechi's contributions to understanding social movements in Latin America. As one of the foremost writers and analysts on social movements in the region, Zibechi has influenced activists, social movement participants, writers, thinkers, and journalists around the globe. The nine books he has written have been translated into six different languages including French, Italian, Turkish, Greek, German, and now English. His articles have appeared in over a dozen languages, and he has given talks and participated in conferences in nearly twenty countries across Latin America, Europe, and beyond.

Zibechi's analysis and focus resonates with a growing number of people concerned with social change from below. Central to much of his writing has been the anti-capitalist relations within movements; how territories of resistance and autonomy exist outside of dominant economic, political, and social models; popular assemblies, and community decision making, relations and actions that build a better world outside the taking of state power.

Like his writing, Zibechi's activism, work, and experience has traversed much geographical and historical ground. As a student in Uruguay from 1969 to 1973, he was a participant of the Frente Estudiantil Revolucionario (Revolutionary Student Front), a student movement linked to the Movimiento de Liberación Nacional Tupamaros (Tupamaros National Liberation Movement). He participated in movements against the dictatorship in Uruguay, and went into exile in Madrid, Spain in 1976, where he was active in the Communist Movement (a Maoist, feminist, and pacifist collective at the time) in rural literacy and anti-military work. In the 1980s he became acquainted first-hand with the liberation movements in Central America, and wrote for various newspapers including *Página Abierta*, *Egin*, *Liberación* and *Página/12* in Argentina and *Mate Amargo* in Uruguay.

From 1986 onward he has traveled and worked throughout all of Latin America as a writer and activist. Zibechi is now an international analyst at one of the best weekly publications in Latin America, *La Brecha*, and regularly contributes to the *Americas Program*, *La Jornada*, and many other publications. In 2003, he won the José Marti Journalism Award for *Genealogy of the Revolt, Argentina: Society in Movement*, a book on the social movements in Argentina during that country's uprising and crisis in 2001. He is the author of many books, including most recently, *Territories in Resistance: Political Cartography of the Latin American Urban Peripheries*. In addition, he is currently a lecturer and researcher on social movements at the Multiversidad Franciscana de América Latina (Fransiscan Multiversity of Latin America), and participates in popular seminars on various topics with social movement groups around the region.

As readers, we are lucky that such a brilliant thinker is also an engaging and accessible writer. In an eloquent arrangement of history, theory, analysis, and reporting, Zibechi offers unique ways of understanding social change. The transformational capacity of his work is not limited to our perceptions; by presenting new ways of seeing, we're also provided with fresh, empowering ways of changing the world we live in.

Zibechi artfully transmits the views of great philosophers, economists, and theorists to his work without bogging the writing down with academic jargon. In his articles and various books, whether writing about the Mapuche in Chile, the Zapatistas, or the Argentine *piqueteros*, unconventional sources are drawn from and under-reported news shared. His writing, like the movements he writes about, is horizontal and participatory; it draws predominantly from the voices and views of those most affected or involved.

Through much of his writing one feels a strain of hope; not some misleading tonic or pair of rose-colored glasses, but hope that embraces the challenges inherent in possibility, the work necessary for liberation, and the self-determination of people over parties, governments, and doctrines.

As Zibechi writes in *Genealogy of the Revolt*, "To defend the new world implies expanding it, deepening it, enriching it." With the publication of *Dispersing Power* in English, this new world has expanded.

Foreword to the German edition

by John Holloway

If you think Bolivia is a far off country, forget it. Don't bother to read this book. Better give it to a friend.

This is a book about you. About your hopes and fears, about the possibilities of living, even of surviving. *De te fabula narratur*, dear reader, and do not forget it as you plunge into the revolt in Bolivia.

Time has done a somersault. Bolivia used to be seen as a backward, underdeveloped country which could hope, if it was lucky, to attain the development of a country like Germany one day in the future. Perhaps even now there are some people who still think like that. But, as the disintegration of the capitalist world becomes more and more obvious, more and more frightening, the flow of time-hope-space is reversed. For more and more Europeans, Latin America has become the land of hope. And now, as we read of the movements in Bolivia, we say not "poor people, have they any hope of catching up with us?" but rather "how wonderful! Can we in Germany (or wherever) possibly hope to do something like that? Can we ever aspire to act like the people of Cochabamba or El Alto?" On the answer to this simple question hangs the future of the world.

There is a turn in the flow of inspiration and of understanding. This was announced by Subcomandante Marcos when, at the end of an interview for an Italian video in 1995, he was asked what Europeans could do to support the Zapatistas and he replied, "the best thing you can do is revolt in your own countries and when we have finished here we shall come over and help you." But of course the flow of help and thought and inspiration has not had to wait for the successful completion of the Zapatista and other revolts in Latin America. The rebels of the world, but especially of Europe, have flocked to Chiapas, to Argentina, to Venezuela and to Bolivia, sometimes just to see and romanticize, but very often to admire, to help and above all to learn from the experiences there.

Raúl Zibechi goes to Bolivia to learn. Like us, he goes with questions, questions that stretch far beyond the borders of Bolivia. How do we change the world and create a different one? How do we get rid of capitalism? How do we create a society based on dignity? What is the role of the state and what are the possibilities of changing society through anti-state movements? What is an anti-state movement? What does "anti-state" mean in the details of everyday practice? Can an anti-state movement sustain itself over time without becoming institutionalized? How can we conceive of a community-based movement within the city? Not all of these questions are made explicit, but it is clear that Zibechi, an Uruguayan academic and journalist who has written very widely and influentially on the new wave of anti-systemic struggles in Latin America, takes with him all the most important practical and theoretical questions that have risen from the struggles in Latin America and the world in the last fifteen years or so. He takes these questions and brings them to life by examining them through the experience of El Alto, the Aymara city just outside La Paz which was the center of the social revolts of the first five years of this century.

Zibechi takes us to the city. This is important. The Zapatista movement here in Mexico has been an enormous source of inspiration in all the world for the last fifteen years. But the Zapatistas of Chiapas are peasants: they live basically by cultivating their own lands and they are supported by tightly knit communities. The question for us who are not peasants is how we create an urban Zapatismo. How can we create autonomous anti-capitalist, anti-state spaces or moments in the city? El Alto offers us many suggestions. One of the central arguments of Zibechi's analysis is that the communities which served as the basis of the revolt in El Alto are not a reproduction of the rural communities from which many of the inhabitants came but a specifically urban phenomenon, forms of mutual support and collective organization arising from the specific problems of living in a difficult urban environment.

These forms of support and organization are woven in the practice of everyday life. Here is the real strength of the revolt. The real forces for social change are not where they appear to be. They are not in the institutions nor in the parties but in the daily contact between people, the daily weaving of social interactions that are not just necessary for survival but the basis of life. It is from this non-visible level that revolt arises, and the strength of the revolt will depend upon its remaining within that daily weaving of the community. The key to the success of the Bolivian revolt is that it is anti-state: not just in the sense that the people rose up against the state and stopped it from implementing its plans, but in the much more profound sense that it runs counter to the separation that the state embodies. Where the state separates people, separates leaders from masses, separates the political from the economic, the public from the private and so on, the struggle in Bolivia constantly resists this separation and binds all collective action firmly into the community. The struggle is the constant creation and recreation of the community—a crucial point too often forgotten by academics and activists.

Asymmetry is at the core of Zibechi's story. We oppose capitalism by being unlike it, we fight the state by being something else. From the Bolivian experience we learn that this is realistic. The Bolivians overthrew the old regime not by elections, not by parties, but simply by pitching the strength of the community against that of the state. And this "something else" that we throw against capital, this community that we create and recreate through struggle, is potentially the embryo of another society. I say "potentially" because there is no certainty in this: Zibechi is very aware of the contradictions of the process and warns that the anti-state uprising, like so many revolutions before it, can end up strengthening the state it opposes. And yet, the study of El Alto shows us the force and everyday practicality of that other world that does not yet exist, and exists not yet, as struggle.

The future of humanity depends now on our being able to bring to life within the old, rotten and increasingly violent capitalism, flashes, intimations, anticipations, fragments of the world of dignity that we want to create. That is what the people of El Alto are doing and, by showing the way, they hurl a challenge at us.

The book is beautiful, exciting, stimulating: for me it is a great honor to be associated with it in this way. Do read it and also give it your friends.

John Holloway
Puebla, Mexico, 11 January 2009

Introduction

> When the subjects have become autonomous producers of wealth, knowledge, and cooperation, without need of external command, when they organize production itself and social reproduction, there is no reason for an overarching, sovereign power external to their own power.
>
> *Antonio Negri and Michael Hardt*
> The Labor of Dionysus: A Critique of the State-Form

The cycle of struggle and insurrection instigated by the Bolivian people in the year 2000 is the most profound "revolution within the revolution" since the Zapatista uprising of 1994. People all over the continent view the struggles taking place in Bolivia as an essential reference point and inspiration for those of us seeking social emancipation. And just as Zapatismo shed light on a new way of doing politics beyond the state in the 1990s, the Bolivian movements show us that it is not only desirable to build power beyond the state, but also possible. Or in other words: not every power need be a separate body above society. It is possible to build the other world we long for without going through that which has always been a nightmare for libertarians throughout history, beginning with Karl Marx: the state.

Beginning in 1989, the popular sectors and Indian peoples of Latin America have led revolts and uprisings that have put the neoliberal model on the defensive. The Caracazo [Caracas insurrection] of 1989 and rebellions of the Ecuadorian Indians from 1990 onwards showed that it was possible to resist and go on the offensive, from the grassroots rural communities and poor, urban neighborhoods. These insurrections played an important role in the de-legitimization of the party-based system that electoral democracy has become.

Zapatismo has illuminated the continent and the world since 1994 with an armed uprising that seeks not to seize power but to build a new world, and shows the importance of building communal, municipal, and regional autonomy, from below. More recently, Zapatismo has been attempting to expand throughout Mexico, propagating a political culture that is premised on listening as a foundation for doing non-institutional politics from below. With their Good Government Councils, the Zapatistas have taught us that it is possible —

1

at least on a small scale—to build non-bureaucratic forms of power, based on the rotation of representatives, that go beyond conventional state practices.

The landless movement in Brazil, Sem Terra (MST), has shown the importance of land reform emerging from the *llano* [plains], and has not only become the most important social movement in the country but now also works with poor youth in large cities in order to kick-start the movement against "leftist neoliberalism."

The *piquetero* [picketers] movement moved the epicenter of the Argentinean struggle from the smaller to the larger cities and from workers to the unemployed and those marginalized by neoliberalism. The popular insurrection of December 19–20, 2001, suggests that it is possible to fight and win without formal structures or designated leaders—without a vanguard party, without the political leaders—and that the organization does not have to be a tombstone that weighs down on the popular sectors. Instead, the movement can take as a starting point that which already exists in the daily lives of the poorest and expand, improve, and intensify from there.

What does the Bolivian struggle bring to the people of Latin America who seek to create a new world? The water and gas "wars" in 2000 and 2003 share some traits with other struggles on the continent like, for example, the lack of vanguards and leadership structures, or the ability to launch victorious insurgencies without any institution (workers, or farmers, union, or political party)—without those on top and those at the bottom. These struggles were won without the traditional division between the leaders and the led. The Bolivian experience also resembles other struggles on the continent in the sense that it was enough for them to draw from that which already exists in order to struggle and win: basically, the rural communities or *ayllus*,[1] and the urban communities and local neighborhood councils. The "organizations" that carry forward the struggles and insurrections are the same "organizations" embedded and submerged in the everyday life of the people, and this is one of the new features of the movements (which are always social and political) of our region. I think it is necessary to elaborate on this point.

Revolution is the midwife of history. Marx's phrase sums up a conception of revolution that has been buried by the Marxists. However, Marx was always faithful to this way of looking at social change, in which the revolutionary act of giving birth to a new world is just a short step in a long process of creating that other world.

---

1   Translator's note: *Ayllu* is a word in the Aymara language referring to a network of families in a given area. It is a pre-Conquest indigenous local government model existing across the Andes region of South America, particularly in Bolivia.

Revolution helps give birth to the new world, but it does not create it. This new world already exists in a certain stage of development and that is why, in order to continue growing, it needs to be delivered by an act of force: the revolution. I feel that what is happening within the social movements is the formation of "another world," one that is not only new but also different from the present one, based on a different logic of construction. This parallels Marx's reflections on the Paris Commune. "The workers," he said, "have no ready-made utopias to introduce *par decret du peuple*[2]. They have no ideals to realize, but to set free the elements of the new society with which old collapsing bourgeois society itself is pregnant."

Allow me to dwell on "to set free," because I think it points to a pivotal element that runs through Marx's entire theory of production. For Marx, communism exists as a potential within capitalist society. He is very clear about this in the *Communist Manifesto* when he discusses the transition from feudalism to capitalism and emphasizes how bourgeois society was born in the bowels of the feudal society. The same, he anticipates, will happen in the transition from capitalism to communism. The new society is not a place that one arrives; it is not something to be conquered and therefore is not out there; and it is even less something implanted. The image that Marx offers us of revolutionary change is that of a latent power that lies dormant within the world of the oppressed, and grows out like a flower. This is why he uses the expression "to set free."

Marx did not use the word "spontaneity" or "spontaneous,"[3] which Kautsky introduced and Lenin later employed, in his state-centric drift. Marx only used the adjectives *selbständig* (alone, on its own initiative) and *eigentümlich* (own / inherent) — or in other words, what exists in and of itself. His work is permeated by the idea of the *self-activity* of the workers and by the use of the term "naturally" to refer to how this activity arises. He affirmed, beyond any doubt, that the concentration of workers caused by the development of capitalism creates the conditions for their unity, based on self-education, and argued that this unity would erode the basis of bourgeois domination: competition between workers. Notice how he finds within the class not only the weaknesses that oppress them but also the powers that free them.

I maintain that the idea "to set free," and the concepts of "self-activity" and "self-organization," all derive from the same conception

---

2   Karl Marx, *La guerra civil en Francia*, Manifiesto del Consejo General de la Asociación Internacional de los Trabajadores (Moscow: Editorial Progreso, 1980), 69.

3   Daniel Guerin, *Rosa Luxemburgo o la espontaneidad revolucionaria* (Buenos Aires: Anarres, 2003), 15.

of the world and social change. It is one based on the idea that these processes occur *naturally*—a word Marx used himself—or, by themselves: that is, as a result of their own internal dynamics.

The internal dynamic of social struggle weaves social relations among the oppressed, as a means of ensuring survival in the first place, both materially and spiritually. With time and the decline of the dominant system, a new world grows upon the basis of these relations or, better said, a different world from the hegemonic. So much so that, eventually, society takes the form of a sea of "new" social relations amid a few islands of the "old" social relations—essentially, statist relations.

Twentieth-century history is full of births of worlds that embody "old" social relations. This tumultuous reality has brought disastrous consequences: in general, revolutions have not given birth to new worlds, though revolutionaries have tried to build them with the state apparatus. Although a good many revolutions have improved people's living conditions, which is certainly an important achievement, they have not been able to create new worlds. Despite the unimpeachable goodwill of so many revolutionaries, the fact remains that the state is not the appropriate tool for creating emancipatory social relations. This is a contested topic, and a point from which an abundant literature has emerged.

From this perspective, the most revolutionary thing we can do is strive to create new social relationships within our own territories—relationships that are born of the struggle, and are maintained and expanded by it.

• • • • • • • • • • • • •

In Bolivia, as in other countries in the Americas, a wholly new trajectory began on January 22, 2006 (the date of the inauguration of the MAS government led by Evo Morales), which presented an unprecedented challenge to Bolivian social movements. In some countries, movements have been weakened by the ascendancy of progressive forces into government, whether because they were co-opted or isolated. We should not overlook these experiences, but instead draw lessons from them in order to avoid the disarticulation of sectors of the struggle. At the moment, left and progressive governments are becoming a real possibility across the Americas and this raises unique problems for grassroots movements. How the movements relate to these governments will be critical in the coming years. The relationship between the two may produce a re-legitimization of the state and the neoliberal model with minimal changes or, conversely, it may allow those forces struggling to build another world to advance anew.

The political, social, and economic scenario does not affect the movement's potency. It conditions its expansion, multiplication, and proliferation, but the potency remains intact, or not, depending on other variables that do not relate strictly to the political scenario. Among these variables, perhaps the most decisive is how the people who make up the movement relate to their own potencies: if they connect with them, cultivate them, intensify them, and convert their potency as a movement into means to achieve certain ends.

Critics point out the limits of the social movements. We are told that the movements are good for weakening or overthrowing governments, for mobilizing society, or for delegitimizing the neoliberal model, but that they lack the "other half"—the ability to strategize, to lead, or to seize the state in order to implement their programs.

From this point of view, there are only two ways of doing politics: based upon limits or based upon people's power. Operating from within the limits implies privileging what we cannot do. It implies putting ourselves in a position of incapacity—like putting ourselves into a hole that "someone else" will get us out of, or so we hope. Setting limitations is to place in the forefront what movements have been unable to do. This attitude has several variants: from those who are banking on the state, whether they advocate establishing alliances with the government directly or through various other channels, to those who submit to the state altogether. At the most grassroots extreme, there are those who choose to "articulate" the various movements so that they will be coherent and have the capacity to influence the political agenda, thereby rendering the mobilizations' pressure more effective. As is evident, these are two versions of the same project: the mobilized society is no longer the subject responsible for the changes—this role is passed on to the state, or the organization/party, or various combinations of both. For those working in this spirit, "the political scenario is everything."

In effect, the political scenario is quantity, while potency is quality. But one cannot be transmuted into the other. It is natural that the question about the usefulness of potency arises from the state-centered gaze. Like emancipation, this kind of power is not useful, it cannot transform itself into exchange value on the altar of the political market. Worse still, it only has use value for those who live it, feel it, practice it. For this reason, the political and social left does not usually extol emancipatory power in the great liturgies that they believe bring about change. And this applies as much to the party congresses as to the social forums.

To make matters worse, it is not possible nor desirable "to define it." We can only recognize it as a *hic Rhodus, hic salta* of Marx. Because what we call potency relates to the experience of human relationships that men and women in movement establish with each other and others—relationships that, individually and collectively, are formed through suffering. "Potency is born of suffering," says Negri.[4] Even more, he states that "all major subject groups are formed from suffering, at least those who fight against the expropriation of the time of life decreed by power." But it is impossible to explain suffering, or to convey it, only to share it; because "it goes beyond logic, rationality, language," it is then, "*a key that opens the door to the community.*"[5]

In this sense we can say, yes, potency can change the people, and change each and every one of us. But only to the extent in which we participate in those relationships—not so much in the movements as institutions, but *in* movement. It is not the ritual demonstrations and marches that change people; but certainly, in some cases, street actions can embody the potencies of change. Something like what happened on December 19–20, and the memorable days of the Water War and October 2003 in Bolivia.

Subcomandante Insurgente Marcos reminds us that "below, to learn is to grow." But he warns that "the seeds from below never yield their harvest immediately."[6] In that manner, Zapatismo cautions us to heed counsel on two things: first, the importance of learning collectively, of making learning an axis of the movement; and, secondly, to deal with the notion of time differently, to depend on internal time rather than the system's time. But this means eliminating the instrumentalism of the means. There is not the slightest difference between ends and means; as Marcos says, the end is in the means.

During the best experiences one can sense a tension to overcome limits. If this tension—which tends to overflow—is the potency of the movements, it seems clear that the political scenario does not affect it. At that stage, the tension dissolves the internal and external. The tension goes to the limit (emancipation), but has no limits or limitations, except that of the tension itself. So potency is never realized, it is a thing that does not materialize, it is always the unfinished becoming. It tends toward the autonomous, because it only depends on itself. Potency expands as it forms and creates relationships—which are manifestations of emancipatory power. It is the only thing we can call power, and it depends only on itself. To enhance, to strengthen, is therefore to deepen the fabric of relations to avoid freezing them into forms of domination.

• • • • • • • • • • • •

4   Antonio Negri, *Job: la fuerza del esclavo* (Buenos Aires: Paidós, 2003), 147.

5   Ibid., 161, italics in the original.

6   Subcomandante Insurgente Marcos, "La velocidad del sueño (III): Pies desnudos" (In *Rebeldía* No. 24, México: October 2004), 14.

The Aymara experience is not only linked with the continental struggles but it also adds something substantial—the construction of actual non-state powers. By this, I am referring to powers that are not separated from or splintered off from society. Powers that do not form a separate elite that makes decisions or leads struggles or resolves internal conflicts. If the state is the monopoly of physical coercion exercised by a body that separate from society (a civil and military bureaucracy), in the Aymara world this capacity is distributed and dispersed throughout the social body and ultimately subject to assemblies in the countryside and the city.

The capacity to build non-state power—decentralized and dispersed—links the Aymara process with the Zapatista (the Good Government Councils), and both represent a vital contribution to emancipation, despite their differences and particularities. One could say that the construction of these powers is explicit in Chiapas and implicit in the barracks and other communal forms in the Aymara Altiplano. This is mostly due to the absence of territorial control among Aymara, although at base similar tensions and aspirations reside.

The non-state powers of the Aymara were born in territories in which the community machine operates: social mechanisms that are de-territorialized and "de-communalized" in order to be used by society in movement as non-state forms of mobilization and to create spaces where—far beyond mere rhetoric—the dictum "to lead by obeying" functions. These are the mechanisms that have enabled Aymara society and other social sectors in Bolivia to unleash powerful mobilizations that have toppled two presidents and defeated the neoliberal project without creating state structures. Now is not the time to think of what will happen in the coming years. The best scenario, the most desirable, is that the new government will be the bearer and voice of change without disempowering the social movements and that they, the social movements, will remain the key players. However, experiences such as those in Argentina—where many of the movements were co-opted by Néstor Kirchner's progressive government—should alert us to the dangers of seduction by the state when it is in the hands of people connected to the movements.

For those of us who struggle for emancipation, the central and critical challenges are not from above but from below. There is no point in blaming the governments or issuing calls of "betrayal." It is a daily task for all of us committed to creating a new world to care for the people's power as the sacred fire of the movement. Let it beat in the heart of the people, a heart woven in popular sociability, without hierarchy or leaders; let it blossom due to the strength of brotherhood; let it be the driving force of any change, the basic fabric and the light of life.

• • • • • • • • • • • • •

This work would not have been possible without the contributions, support, and complicity of many people. I thank from the bottom of my heart those who devoted their time to explaining, in interviews and informal conversations, their views on a wide range of themes related to their experience of the social movements. Thanks to Alvaro García Linera, who always brings clarity and vision; Bruno Rojas, for his statistical information about El Alto; to Félix Patzi, for revealing to me the particular worldview of the Aymara as an alternative to capitalism; and to Pablo Mamani Ramírez for introducing me at the Public University of El Alto and explaining in detail how the local committees operate. Silvia Rivera added her brilliant intellectual disposition, as a feminist and a committed, sensitive woman, one who transforms discussions into moments of inspiration and freshness. And thanks to Mujeres Creando, for contributing an intransigent rebelliousness that prompts us, though provocation and making us feel uncomfortable, to think.

In Cochabamba, I shared meals, discussions, and workshops in an atmosphere of brotherhood with Oscar Olivera, Giselle, Claudia, Marcelo, and Marcela. Dunia enabled me to participate in a fruitful meeting with workers at home. Thanks to Oscar Fernandez and Omar, I had the opportunity to attend meetings of the heroic irrigation valley, where three decades ago the first roadblocks were born in an exciting time "irrigated" by abundant and delicious *chicha*. Abraham Grandidier undertook tremendous efforts to make me understand the incredible experience of water cooperatives in the southern zone of Cochabamba.

In El Alto, the members of Youth of October (Abraham, Elijah Uvalde, Alex, and Johnny) shared their experiences and, in particular, the history of public plazas as forums for non-institutional discussion and training, which will have the time and opportunity to consolidate. Marco and Julio Mamani Quispe Conde shared their expansive knowledge of the past and present of the social movement in El Alto. Juan Carlos Condori offered his experience in the Warisata school and the struggle of the Aymara peasant movement in the area of Achacachi.

The continuous exchange with Colectivo Situaciones over the years remains a source of inspiration and has been instrumental in several sections of this work. The contributions of Raquel Gutiérrez Aguilar, her deep commitment and pervasive human wit and creativity, are present throughout this text. Luis Gomez is in many ways the co-author of this book: although he is absolved of all responsibility for the final result, it could not have been born and taken shape without his generous and selfless assistance, companionship, and stimulation. I hope to live up to his commitment to strengthening the brotherhood forged during the investigation.

Pola and Augustine, as always, are a presence on every page.

CHAPTER 1

The Community as Social Machine

During moments of insurrection, mobilizations dissolve both state and social movement institutions. Societies in movement, articulated from within quotidian patterns, open fissures in the mechanisms of domination, shred the fabric of social control, and disperse institutions. In short, societies in movement expose social fault lines, which are uncovered as society shifts away from its previous location. Times in which there is an intensely creative outpouring—during which social groups release huge amounts of energy—act like a bolt of lightning capable of illuminating subterranean molecular cooperation, hidden by the veil of everyday inertias that are imposed in time and space through domination and subordination.

To take lightning—insurrectional—moments as epistemological moments is to privilege the transience of the movement and, above all, its intensity, in order to encounter what lies behind and below the established forms. During the uprising, shadowed areas (that is, the margins in the eyes of the state) are illumined, albeit fleetingly. The insurgency is a moment of rupture in which subjects display their capacities, their power as a capacity to do, and deploy them, revealing aspects hidden in moments of repose, when there is little collective activity.

Elites and masses mobilize in completely different ways, particularly in colonial societies. The former do so vertically, closely linked to the institutions; social action takes place in a "cautious and controlled" manner and its high point comes in electoral contests. However, the mobilization of the poor is, on the contrary, horizontal, more spontaneous and based "on the traditional kinship and territoriality or associations of class" that appear linked to the insurgency.[1] The characteristics of a horizontal mobilization enable it to reveal the hidden aspects of cooperation that, upon bursting forth, displays what is implicit. In short, the space-time of the uprising reveals the internal space-time that is invisible to us (and even to the actors themselves) in the everyday reality of domination. To put it differently, popular sectors only discover their internal power when it is unleashed.

---

1   Ranahit Guha, *Las voces de la historia* (Barcelona: Crítica, 2002), 37.

This is what happened during the uprisings in Cochabamba in early 2000 and in the highlands and the Aymara city of El Alto. In April and September–October 2000, September–October 2003, and May–June 2005, the blockades of roads and highways—which crystallized radical social activity—fragmented the territory over which the state exercised its authority. Indeed, authority is delegitimized when the insurgency appears on the stage, in the public arena, and a different project is born, existing through the dispersion of state institutions.

The manifold deployment of the capacity to act from below disarticulates the institutional. How is it that this social machinery is capable of such dismissal and dispersion? What intrinsic characteristics confer such potentialities? One, which we track throughout this work, consists of the formation of non-state powers, meaning power distributed somewhat evenly throughout the social fabric and political powers not separated from the society from which they are born. During the insurrection, we see how the social body (the rural and urban communities) are power structures without specialized bodies, power in movement—without power over the collective. During the great movements, social power is intensified in communities, neighborhoods, towns, and cities; we see hundreds of thousands, millions, becoming capable through their everyday lives of doing things that seemed quite impossible beforehand.

Nor can it be said that this energy is only unleashed during the big mobilizations. Collective energies reappear in an infinity of instances, especially in disaster situations or those in which an individual alone cannot solve the problem. Does this mean that they are "sleeping" energies that wake up when needed? Or, conversely, are they energies that are being used and recreated within the intimacy of the family or neighborhood, in the gaps of everyday life? The questions accumulate, and we already know that many do not have simple answers. We cannot ignore the fact that—even in the world of the oppressed, in this case that of the urban and rural Aymara—relations with the state do exist and indeed gain strength when the waters of social rebellion are calmed. What happens to these collective energies and the non-state powers they encourage, when insurrectional times give way to periods of tranquility? Can non-state powers be institutionalized? How, in which spaces, and during what time? Or, to pose a different question, how can non state relations be changed into the natural relations of the present society? It interests us to know how social relations within the state give way to non-state social relations; how that path is reversed; and, especially, how both dynamics coexist in the same space-time.

• • • • • • • • • • • •

For ten or twelve days in October 2003, residents of El Alto, organized through neighborhood councils and other means, operated as a neighborhood government that supplanted the delegitimized and absent state. Descriptions of the insurgency all indicate that there was no single organization or leadership, and that actions were carried out directly by the residents of the neighborhoods, overriding all other institutions and organizations, even the ones created by them beforehand. Even the local councils, the most "grassroots" organizations of the El Alto movement, did not lead the mobilization but acted as "structures of territorial identity within which other kinds of loyalties, organizational networks, solidarities, and initiatives are deployed in an autonomous manner above and, in some cases, outside of the authority of the neighborhood council."[2]

Although the local councils sometimes called the meetings, in most cases these were symbolic for the residents and, in fact as institutions, they did not exercise great influence over neighborhood actions. All social leadership was revolved, and those who made the decisions were "the neighbors themselves in a form of neighborhood micro-governments."[3] One author, who also participated in his local neighborhood council, says that during the uprising "each neighborhood stands as a small power" and that the fight is "to occupy and defend neighborhood territories."[4] In these areas, there is very active participation from all ages and genders, in which "their own internal strengths must be set in motion in order to confront the external conflicts." It is, in short, putting "into practice the everyday, face-to-face social relationships between each and everyone."[5] According to all the testimonies and analyses, organization was improvised and spontaneous. Without planning, and with territorial control based on trenches and barricades, everyone quickly agreed to take turns doing guard duty at the blockades. The entire population was mobilized—organized by block, by street, by committee—and, as pointed out by the president of the Santiago II zone, "without need for compulsory agreements."[6]

Actions of this magnitude cannot be consummated without the existence of a dense network of relationships between people—relationships that are also forms of organization. The problem is that we are unwilling to consider that in everyday life the relationships

2   Alvaro García Linera, *Sociología de los movimientos sociales en Bolivia* (La Paz: Oxfam-Diakonía, 2004), 606.

3   Pablo Mamani Ramírez, *Los microgobiernos barriales en el levantamiento de la ciudad de El Alto* (Unpublished, 2004), 57.

4   Ibid., 54.

5   Ibid., 52.

6   Ibid., 62.

between neighbors, between friends, between comrades, or between family, are as important as those of the union, the party, or even the state itself. In the dominant imagination, organization is understood to mean the institutionalized and also, therefore, hierarchical—visible and clearly identifiable. Established relations, codified through formal agreements, are often more important in Western culture then those loyalties woven by informal ties. In short, association (where the bonds of rationality turn people into means for the purpose of achieving an end) is usually considered more important than community (woven at base on subjective relationships in which the ends are the people). Reality suggests otherwise: community-based relationships have an enormous power and movements or insurgencies are forged in the bosom of those relationships—such as that of October 2003 in El Alto. As a first step, we will try to show that communities were born in El Alto, not just *one* but many El Alto communities or, to put it differently, subjective links in which the participants are all one.

Community does not merely exist, it is made. It is not an institution, not even an organization, but a way to make links between people. But it is less important to define the community than to see how it works. Communities exist and indeed pre-dated the Bolivian social movement. But there is no essential community, no abstract and general community identity. There is a communal system that is expressed in economic and political forms: "the collective ownership of resources and the private management or usufruct of them."[7] The communal system is further expressed by collective deliberation and the rotation of representatives (so that control of the material resources or sovereignty is not alienated from the community), where the representative is appointed not to command but "simply to organize the course of the collective will."[8] Although the community is born in rural indigenous societies that have "no separation between the distinct fields (economic, political, and cultural, etc.) and function as a single system," the characteristics of the communal system are universal.[9]

The economy of the communal system—according to Félix Patzi—excludes the exploitation or appropriation of the work of others, because the collective goods are usufructuary in private and familial form. Therefore, alienated labor does not exist, as the family and its members control modes and rates of production, and are not

---

7   Félix Patzi, *Sistema comunal, una propuesta alternativa al sistema liberal* (La Paz: CEA, 2004), 171.

8   Raquel Gutiérrez, *Forma comunal y forma liberal de la política* (La Paz: Comuna, 2000), 71.

9   Félix Patzi, 171.

subject to control other than that of the community. How much and how each family works is up to each family unit to decide, so long as it is not detrimental to the others. In this way there is no exploitation and alienation, at least for adult males (the previous statement cannot be extended to women and children because forms of oppression and subordination still exist in the communities). To prevent people from prospering at the expense of others, there is a "regulatory system at political and cultural level," within the *ayllu economic system*.[10]

In the sphere of political power, the figure of community representative is different from what we know in traditional politics. Weber distinguishes "non-authoritarian administrations" from "administrations of representatives." The first are communities where sovereignty is not separate from society and operates as a kind of direct democracy. In the latter, the figure of the representative negates the relationship of solidarity, as the people are formed together as a group as a means to achieve certain ends.[11] The description he makes of representation as domination is particularly relevant to the relationship between social movements and political parties:

> Immediate democracy and government by notables exist in their genuine forms, free from *herrschaft* (domination), only so long as parties which contend with each other and attempt to appropriate office do not develop on a permanent basis. If they do, the leader of the contending and victorious party and his staff constitute a structure of domination, regardless of how they attain power and whether they formally retain the previous mode of administration.[12]

Even in the case of "free representation" in which the representative is "elected" (Weber always uses the term in quotes) "he is not bound by any instructions, but is *master of his own conduct*."[13] In the communal system that kind of autonomy is unthinkable, so the word "representation" is just a semantic loan that, as we shall see, in Aymara logic can be extended to other words such as state.[14] This idea of representation, understood as "to lead by obeying," does not exist in modern Western political logic.

To complete the picture, it is worth pointing out that representation in the community is not voluntary but compulsory and by rotation. Unlike what happens within the liberal framework, the person

---

10   Ibid., 175.

11   Max Weber, *Economía y Sociedad* (Madrid: FCE, 2002), 38.

12   Ibid., 234.

13   Ibid., 236, my emphasis.

14   Interview with Pablo Mamani Ramírez.

elected in the community is not the most capable, or the most learned, or the most intelligent candidate, but simply whoever's turn it happens to be. We are therefore not dealing with a democratic method, but what Patzi defines as "authoritarianism based in consensus."[15] Representation, then, is not elective but a duty satisfied on behalf of the community, given by all if they wish to continue using the communal assets (land, water, and pasture, etc.).

We are dealing with social machinery that prevents the concentration of power or, similarly, prevents the emergence of a separate power from that of the community gathered in assembly. There is no separation between economy and politics or between society and state, "or that is to say, power is in society itself, and the state changes form and becomes another structure of coordination for the representatives to oversee collective decisions."[16]

What we have here is a non-divided society, which is how Clastres portrays primitive societies. For this anthropologist, who lived among the Guayaqui Indians,[17] the state is "the consummate symbol of the social division, as it is a separate organ of political power. From that moment, society divides between those who wield power and those who endure it."[18] A multiplicity of indivisible communities is the salient characteristic of a society without a state; a *"non-ðivision"* that allows them to assert their difference. We can begin to observe this essential feature of the community—which Clastres calls *"non-ðivision"* and Patzi calls "undifferentiated communal systems"[19]—in some cities like El Alto, and it also seems to exist in Cochabamba in relation to the community administration of water. A good example is the non-division manifested during the insurgency: confrontation, even armed, does not require a special body separated from the community. In fact, the same bodies that sustain everyday life sustain the uprising (the neighborhood assemblies in the local councils of El Alto). The rotation of tasks and the obligatory character assures everyday community life—which we will look at in more detail later— just as it guaranteed the task of blocking roads and streets. The appearance of this type of social mobilization in urban zones indicates that urban communities have been born.

---

15   Félix Patzi, 177.

16   Ibid., 180.

17   Pierre Clastres, French anthropologist and ethnologist, lived a year in the rainforest with Guayaquís, nomadic hunter-gatherers. From that experience—a sort of "militant research"—he prepared a report on their daily life: *Crónica de los indios guayaquís*, (Barcelona: Alta Fulla, 2001.)

18   Pierre Clastres, *Arqueología de la violencia* (Buenos Aires: FCE, 2004), 74–75.

19   Félix Patzi, ibid., 181.

The issue is relevant given that the strength of the Aymara rebellion now rests in cities, particularly El Alto. If the characteristics of the communal system were valid only in rural areas, where indigenous society functions, it would be impossible to go beyond established ways of doing institutional politics through the state. One of the central theses of this work is that communities have been formed in cities like El Alto that are different from those of the countryside, but communities nonetheless. On this point, there seems to be a reluctance to acknowledge that in some cities there are community relations that shape anti-systemic movements and profoundly change their characteristics. An excellent work on the Bolivian social movement[20] points out that the Unique Confederation of Rural Laborers of Bolivia (Confederación Sindical Única de Trabajadores Campesinos de Bolivia, CSUTCB) —whose capacity for action lies within the communities— is a social movement that "not only mobilizes a part of society, but generates a distinct society, a new set social relations, with non-capitalist forms of working, and modes of organization, meaning, representation, and political authority that are completely different from that of the dominant society."[21] Thus, the mobilization of the rural community represents a social movement, or a society in movement.

However, when analyzing the El Alto movement, this investigation also makes use of other categories, highlighting the presence of "everyday neighborhood networks" or "neighborhood block groups," to explain the density and intensity of the mobilization.[22] Although García Linera assumes that local councils regulate everyday life "in a similar way as agricultural unions,"[23] and constantly refers to the similarities between the action in El Alto and that of rural communities, he prioritizes the concept of networks (a concept born in the first world in a different context and a point of reference for other kinds of movements) and he rules out the existence of urban communities.[24] As a hypothesis developed throughout the work, I will argue that such an analysis frames the community as an institution and not as a relationship, which also occurs in the treatment of social movements.[25]

---

20   Alvaro García Linera.

21   Ibid., 130.

22   Ibid., 590.

23   Ibid., 602.

24   The work refers to the "neighborhood community," a concept that he puts in quotation marks, as he believed that they only "moved" aspects of rural communities to the city of El Alto (García Linera, 601).

25   Although it is not the object of this work to enter into this polemic, it has a relational community character (relations between people and between each other and

Neighborhood Cohesion, a Form of Survival

The urban settlement of the Aymara occurred in three great waves. The first was in La Paz, in relatively central areas surrounding traditional white neighborhoods: Buenos Aires Avenue, the area around San Pedro, and Peru Avenue. These have been economically successful and have formed an Aymara "bourgeoisie."[26] The second wave settled on the hillsides of La Paz, and this generation has produced the intellectual elite that made up the Katarismo movement. The third wave began with the onset of neoliberalism in 1985 and those from this period have had few opportunities, with many living in extreme poverty. "That is the ninety percent of the population of the city of El Alto that is almost entirely employed in retail trade... they are the ones reviving communal civilization in the neighborhoods and in the various trade unions,"[27] states Aymara sociologist Félix Patzi. In connection with the recent experience of the social movement, he also observes that this "is the part of the population that will determine the course of the contemporary indigenous struggle."[28]

In fact, most of the El Alto population arrived in the city after 1985. We can see the statistics: in 1950 there were 11,000 inhabitants and by 1960 there were approximately 30,000; in 1976 El Alto had 96,000 residents; in 1985 there were 307,000; in 2001 it reached 650,000; and by 2005 it was close to 800,000. Almost ninety percent of the current population arrived after 1976, and two-thirds arrived after 1985. In sum, we can say that the El Alto population settled in the city en masse in the space of one generation. They all came together and for the same reason: they were expelled by the neoliberal model which is actually a kind of neo-colonialism, re-colonizing the country and its people.

The Aymara did not simply migrate from rural areas to El Alto with a "community consciousness" that they "revived" upon arrival. On the contrary, they created another type of community—they re-

---

the surroundings). In the same sense, it considers the social movements from a point of view that privileges the relational and the disengagement aspect of the movement: "Every social movement configures itself starting with those who break the inertia and mobilize themselves, which is to say, they change place, refusing to stay put in the place where they were historically assigned within a determined social organization, and seek to widen the spaces of expression" (Porto Gonçalves, 2001: 81).

26   The term is provisional and incorrect: one should not apply such concepts to situations very different from which they have arisen. The European bourgeoisie is a result of a long historical process that does not correspond with the experience of the urban Aymara who have become rich via trade and services.

27   Félix Patzi, "Todo lo que caduca merece perecer." in *Memoria testimonial de la guerra del gas* (El Alto: Cáritas-Diocesis, 2003), 7.

28   Ibid.

invented and re-created one. Given the enormous challenges they faced, it is not surprising that the inhabitants of El Alto have been forced to work collectively in order to meet their most basic needs. Collective relations, widespread in the Andean world, operate as a sort of "common sense" to which people continually turn to solve problems big and small, whether in daily life or in the major political events. Collective relationships shape Andean behavior. In the first place, *arriving and setting up en masse in the city was a collective act*, since in many cases (such as for the miners or refugees relocated after a disaster) the decision to leave the places they had inhabited—whether imposed by the state or by capital, because of climatic change or for other reasons—was taken collectively.

In many ways, emigration to El Alto represented a reaction to the very real social and cultural earthquake experienced by Bolivians in the 1980s. The hundreds of thousands of people who suddenly landed in the cold and desolate pampa, as harsh as it was remote, sought and found new lives like survivors of a giant collective shipwreck. That feeling of surviving a tragedy, as well as the poverty and the shared physical space, helped bring cohesion to their muddled and dramatic shared biography, chiseled by the uncertainties and pains of the exodus. It so happened that the enormity of the exodus overwhelmed all the previous societal configurations, from the urban layout to the political and social organizations, and across the board through education, health, water, electricity, sewage, and transportation.

The urban layout of El Alto is atypical and reveals how the population settled. All that remains of the original pattern of the city are the major exit routes: the Viacha, Oruro, Desaguadero, and Copacabana roads, and the large avenues that lead to these roads. Between these routes, there is a set of settlements or urbanizations or neighborhoods that are grafted into a sort of jigsaw puzzle, giving the fabric of the locality a sense of discontinuity even though each unit is homogeneous and has its own ambience. The more than four hundred urbanizations occupied by migrants make up the pieces of this puzzle. On a larger scale, one can differentiate between El Alto North and El Alto South: the first was settled by people from the provinces of Omasuyus, northern Camacho, and generally by those coming from the northern highlands, while the southern area was settled by those from Aroma, Pacajes, and other regions of the southern Altiplano. In this way, the two *parcialidades*[29] found in Andean communities are reproduced.[30]

---

29   In traditional Aymara communities, each *ayllu* is divided into two *parcialidades: aransaya* and *urinsaya*, the upper part and the lower part, representing a concept deeply rooted in the Andean worldview.

30   Interview with Pablo Mamani Ramírez.

The quantitative development of the local councils and the territorial base (grassroots, neighborhood) organizations is a case in point. Up to 1988, they had established 180 local councils, which, given the population of the time (some 360,000 inhabitants) indicates that each had about 2,000 people.[31] By 2004, there were 540 local councils, for a population of about 750,000 inhabitants, signfiying that each had about 1,300 to 1,400 habitants.[32] Although the data is relative, it demonstrates that the density of local councils, proportional to the size of the population, rose. Or to say it in another way, as the population grew the councils became smaller, but they were also stronger—as suggested by the strength of the social movements of the last five years. This seemingly contradictory fact has clear links to the lived experience of the El Alto population in the 1990s. We can postulate that since 1985 emigration to El Alto "communalized" social relations, since it is the mass transfer of whole communities— mining as well as rural—that represents a plebeian migration, with extensive experience of organization and struggle. This large-scale migration redesigned and proletarianized large areas of the city.

By "communalizing," I refer to a process in which social bonds take on a communitarian character, thus strengthening reciprocity, collective ownership of common spaces, "*ayllu* democracy,"[33] and the role of family units in social life, among the most immediate examples. We must understand the decrease in the number of inhabitants per urbanization as a collective choice, making it more difficult for the state and the party system to control the neighborhood communities. Or, seen from below, smaller territorial units facilitate face-to-face community control, thus preventing the formation of bureaucracies and institutions that are separate from the overall neighborhood.

Various academics agree that each settlement has a common history and common problems—that most of the El Alto residents generally share—and an organization that exercises authority over all levels: the local council. Some refer to these neighborhood units as "differentiated urban islets" and some see in them an "enclosure of residents within the boundaries of their neighborhood."[34] The truth is that every neighborhood has its own identity and history that, in

31   Godofredo Sandóval and Fernanda Sostres, *La ciudad prometida* (La Paz: Ildis, 1989), 103.

32   PAR El Alto, *El Alto: 9 aspectos que configuran la ciudad* (La Paz: PAR, 2005), 20.

33   Esteban Alejo Ticona, "El thakhi entre los aymaras y los quechuas o la democracia en los gobiernos comunales." In *Los Andes desde los Andes* (La Paz : Yachaywasi, 2003).

34   Rafael Indaburu, *Evaluación de la ciudad de El Alto* (USAID), 7.

general, the residents project in the name of their neighborhood.[35] The settlements always begin on a vacant lot, and the distinguishing features and internal fabric of each neighborhood typically reflect the history of its formation and the particular problems encountered therein. This is how neighborhoods of former miners, rural farmers, and factory workers arose, each relocated for different reasons. Entire neighborhoods are made up of people coming from the same province, canton, or community. For example, migrants from Warisata and Achacahi make up the neighborhood of Villa Ingenio; miners created Villa Esperanza and Villa Santiago II; those affected by the construction of the airport built Villa Tunari; and factory workers are responsible for Primero de Mayo.[36] With the closure of the mines in 1985, emigration to El Alto intensified:

> After the relocation, more or less in '85, '86, and '87, makeshift tents begin to appear where there had been none before but then they appeared suddenly one December 31 in the Santiago II zone. Afterwards they came to Santa Rosa, which was more dramatic because it was on the edge of the El Alto garbage dump. Tents began to appear in Chalapaqui, and that led to an increase in the settlement, with more and more tents, and then they began to construct simple adobe rooms, and so the miners settled there. They were more or less the disorderly migrations, because usually in El Alto the migrants set up settlements by community—for example, Pacaya is a well-ordered settlement. They bought the land themselves and the community sold it. In these areas, everyone comes from the Pacajes province. It is the same for in Ingenio, there are only people there from Omasuyus.[37]

Emigration and settlement in El Alto are collective acts, determined and executed collectively; as a result, the new settlements tend to be homogeneous in terms of origins. Two very concrete examples of this are those expelled by the construction of the motorway to the city of La Paz, who in turn created Villa Adela, and those affected by flooding in the hills of La Paz in 1986, who created the Aguas de

---

35   Felipe Quispe, "La lucha de los ayllus kataristas hoy." In Fabiola Escárzaga and Raquel Gutiérrez *Movimiento indígena en América Latina: resistencia y proyecto alternativo*, (México: Benemérita Universidad Autónoma de Puebla, 2005).

36   Marco Quispe, *De ch'usa marka a jach'a marka* (El Alto: Plural-Wayna Tambo), 2004.

37   Interview with Julio Mamani Conde.

la Vida urbanization. This neighborhood had moved almost in its entirety to an open field in El Alto in 1986 and created the urbanization "by means of community action," receiving materials from the state (FONVI) and building their homes "by means of communal action."[38]

Those affected by the highway, meanwhile, were moved to the most remote zone of El Alto, where they had to fight—like all residents of El Alto—for access to electricity, water, sewage, housing, and streets. But in this case, there was a series of elements that encouraged unusual unity: "When we had to leave for the city or to go to El Alto we had to line up at five o'clock in the morning, to get to jobs starting at five, six, and seven o'clock in the morning. There was no transport ... so we came to the junction of Viacha from Villa Adela on foot."[39] Something similar happened to the residents of the February 16 neighborhood, the manufacturing area, when there was hardly any transport for La Ceja:

> From here we all went out on foot to Carmen Mercado, and as you see, the path is very dark. Then in the El Carmen market we all grouped together and went there laughing in order to protect us from danger and the criminals. So, we only entered in groups, some came at nine, others at ten and eleven, and the last group at twelve midnight. Only in groups could we enter.[40]

We are dealing with a population of hundreds of thousands of people arriving in the new city at the same time; homogeneous groups of people settling into inhospitable open fields, without the most basic services. To overcome a difficult situation—whose salient features were isolation, danger, and the social earthquake provoked by the implementation of the neoliberal model—the recently arrived residents come together, make decisions, and work collectively. Without a doubt, Aymara traditions play an important role as a *long memory*[41] from which they could extract traditions of communal, collective work.

Multiple factors seem to have inspired the unity of action among El Alto inhabitants. We will look at some of them here without attempting to establish hierarchies. One binding factor is the shared demands, which cut across all neighborhoods and sectors of the population suffering similar hardships and confronting the same problems.

---

38   Marco Quispe, ibid., 28.

39   Ibid., 127.

40   Ibid., 24.

41   Silvia Rivera, *Oprimidos pero no vencidos* (La Paz: Yachaywasi, 2003).

The first marches were for the paving of the Pan-American Highway—they called it the Avenue of the Bombardment—to go to Rio Seco you had to wait an hour or two, and to come back it was the same. There were these clunky old jalopies, not the transport that there is now. First the demand was for electricity and clean water, then for the general hospital and the university. Those have always been the five demands: pave the Pan-American Highway, the hospital, electricity, drinking water, and the university. The first march was in El Alto. It was huge, everyone marched and it was the first blockade carried out by the local councils and the first time that the FEJUVE[42] made a ruckus—it was the year 1987.[43]

However, the unity in the neighborhoods of El Alto seems welded by other factors. In the lines above, we mentioned that they arrived "all together," both symbolically and materially. When discussing those aspects that had united European workers when they came together as a class, British historian Eric Hobsbawm points to two elements that are relevant to this case—social and spatial segregation. Not only were they poor and their lives insecure, but "workers lived in a different way than others, with different life expectations, and in different places." And he adds:

> They brought together, ultimately, the core element of their lives: collectivity, the prevalence of "we" over "I." This provides the movement and their workers' party the force of their conviction that people like them couldn't improve their situation through individual action but only through collective action... But the "we" dominated the "I" not only for instrumental reasons but because the lives of the working class had to be largely public, because of the lack of private spaces.[44]

Hobsbawm concludes by noting that entertainment also had to be public due to the lack of private spaces, from neighborhood parties to football matches and union actions, "life at its most pleasurable moments was a collective experience."[45] At this point, I would draw attention to the unifying role played by deprivation, since for a good proportion of the El Alto inhabitants, life in the new city was consid-

---

42   Federation of Neighborhood Councils in El Alto.
43   Interview with Julio Mamani Conde.
44   Eric Hobsbawm, *Historia del siglo XX* (Barcelona: Crítica, 1995), 308.
45   Ibid.

erably harder than in the mines or in rural communities, where they had lived with a relative comfort.[46]

Furthermore, testimonies speak not only of collective deprivation but also of danger. The extreme conditions of life facilitate the creation of what James Scott calls "communities of destiny."[47] This is something that occurs among groups such as miners, merchant seamen, loggers, and stevedores—groups of workers with a unique predisposition to struggle—who have a high level of internal cohesion as a result of the physical danger of their work. This situation leads to high degrees of camaraderie and cooperation, because "one's life depends on one's co-workers." Secondly, these groups of workers live in relative isolation. Both factors foster a situation marked by homogeneity, mutual dependence, and the relative lack of differentiation and social mobility. In sum, "everyone lives under the same authority, runs the same risks, relates almost exclusively to each other, and depends heavily on mutual aid."[48]

Thirdly, there is the matter of suffering. This is present in all the stories of El Alto inhabitants, beginning from their arrival in the city, to the way they built their homes and neighborhoods, to the events of September–October 2003. Suffering is a fundamental force for the people of El Alto. The biblical book of Job has a close relationship with the power of the Latin American Indian, born in suffering, the daughter of a pain that cannot be explained. Indian power is formed in suffering—which "is a key that opens the door to the community."[49]

Urban Communities

So far we have mentioned the cohesive elements of the El Alto population, but without going into depth about it, because we believe that when we speak of urbanization or neighborhoods organized in local committees, we are dealing with urban communities. Rafael Archondo argues that the city dissolves community control, that it distributes social forces in search of equilibrium. However, he also believes that despite the significant differences between urban and rural areas, "there are very good reasons to suppose that the founda-

---

46   Marco Quispe, ibid.

47   James Scott, *Los dominados y el arte de la resistencia* (México: ERA, 2000), 165.

48   Ibid.

49   Antonio Negri, *Job, la fuerza del esclavo* (Paidós, 2003), 161.

tions are present to restore the Andean logic of reciprocity under the new terms imposed by the urban context."[50]

The fact that the vast majority of the El Alto population works in the informal sector or in family businesses is one of the key elements to understanding why they find similarities to the division of communally held land in the countryside: "Both produce within the family context, are considered non-capitalist, and subsidize the formal sectors."[51] Hence it follows that a discourse based on community values has resonance because they face similar economic challenges in the city, while they can only confront the external challenges on the basis of Andean cultural forms. The stress of urban life means that Andean culture in the city faces challenges very similar to those found in rural areas, so much so that the birth of a social pyramid of large inequalities imposes "the necessity of restoring the Andean logic of reciprocity and redistribution."[52]

For the sociologist Pablo Mamani, head of Sociology at the Public University of El Alto (UPEA) who has lived in El Alto since 1998, "the local councils have similar characteristics as the rural *ayllus* in their structure, logic, territorial dimension, and system of organization."[53] When migrants arrive in the town—anxious, disorganized, lacking in so much—"they need a body, a space for collective decisions, and that becomes a neighborhood council." They also come with great organizational experience from their communities and agricultural or miners' unions, but find that in their new environment, there are greater shortages than in the countryside or in the mine, and that only by organizing together can these problems be resolved. How could individual families, on their own, get electricity or channel the water; build sewers, streets, sidewalks, or public spaces; in a place in which neither the state nor the municipality authorities exist? Mamani poses a key question: in this unknown and hostile space, "who protects them if not the neighborhood council?"

In terms of what binds people together, he argues:

> Here each family has their own property but there are common areas, such as the green area and the school. To sell a lot here, the resident has to go to the neighborhood council, which controls who buys and who sells, like in the *ayllu*. An assessment is made to ascertain if there are any outstanding debts to the committee or other fac-

---

50   Rafael Archondo, *Compadres al micrófono. La resurrección metropolitana del ayllu* (La Paz: Hisbol, 1991), 73.

51   Ibid., 74.

52   Ibid.

53   Interview with Pablo Mamani Ramírez.

tors that might prevent the sale. This is also the space to present a new resident, who offers beer and requests to be received as a new resident.

Nobody is obliged to go to the council if they don't want to, but there is a social sanction if you don't go, such as rumors that the neighbor does not respect the neighborhood or the council, and in order to avoid that, everybody goes, so that they don't have a bad image. In general, one representative from each family attends. In the *ayllu*, elected positions are designated for the family couple. Here it is only the man who is designated but the woman is symbolically the *mama talla* (the wife of an Aymara Community leader), and the man consistently consults the woman and often they assume the leadership when the husband is not around. So, they assume the role symbolically, and sometimes in reality.[54]

Doubtless, the neighborhood councils have similarities to, and differences from, the rural councils and trade unions. They consist of an executive board made up of some fifteen secretariats, of which only four are permanent.[55] To join the Federation of Neighborhood Councils (FEJUVE) one must have a map of the urbanization approved by the mayor's office and it must consist of at least two hundred families, although the criteria are flexible. In order to take the post of leader, one cannot be a real estate speculator, merchant, transportation worker, baker, or leader of a political party; he or she cannot be a "traitor, nor have colluded with dictators," although these requirements are also flexible.[56] Meetings are usually held once a month but sometimes every week; the man usually attends, but often it is the couple who attends. Young people only go when the parents are unable to be present, although in recent years the participation of youth and women has increased. Decisions are taken by vote, but when the issues discussed are very important then consensus must be reached. Each council usually has a small local meeting place where the executive meets and the meetings occur, although many are held in the plaza or on the main street, standing in a circle and sometimes with a table placed in front of attendees, through rain or cold, lasting an hour or two. "Women are placed on one side and men on the other; the women feel comfortable talking amongst themselves, there are two *parcialidades* like in the *ayllu*."[57] In addition to the life of

54   Ibid.
55   Sandóval and Sostres, ibid., 80.
56   Ibid., 82.
57   Interview with Pablo Mamani Ramírez.

the organization, the neighborhood council regulates construction in the neighborhood and sometimes heads production and subsistence projects:

> El Alto is built by its inhabitants. If a water channel has to be dug, each neighbor does his part and the rest is done collectively. In building the school, soccer field, or plaza, each one works or provides materials, so that it is absolutely collective. There are rounds and shifts; the logic is that everyone should participate in the undertaking. There is a lot of pressure to do so and if you don't, you have to explain why, and if not, you must pay a fine. Usually the penalty is merely symbolic. It is said that absence is punishable by a fifty pesos fine, but in reality I don't think it is collected. It's more symbolic.[58]

On the other hand, the councils are a space for the resolution of conflicts between neighbors (quarrels, debts, etc.). Since the option of recourse to the police or the justice system is unthinkable, a resident will put the issue before the executive or assembly, so it can consider the matter. The school councils operate like "a miniature academic government" whose objectives revolve around the regulation and improvement of teaching and to ensure that teachers perform their duties, with "symbolic" sanctions for those who do not attend meetings or activities—although there are those who argue that "the fines are never paid."[59] As for the unions, their primary mission is to make sure that the market stalls operate without the usual conflicts over space and location, and they also raise money in the form of taxes for the Regional Workers Center (Central Obrera Regional, COR). "The owners of the stalls make up the union associations (meat, groceries, bread)," which gives them a lot of power and the ability to convoke the workers, and when there is conflict, "people go to the neighborhood associations, which are the most important organizations with a local presence."[60]

The sociologist Patzi also lives in El Alto and, true to his conception of *the communal system*, he argues that there is no community without the collective management of resources, an element that is, in his opinion, the basis for community cohesion. His reflections on the El Alto social movement raise a key question: Why do movements in El Alto obey the local authorities when they don't have to? Why do the residents comply with the obligation to take turns and attend the marches? Obedience would be normal in a rural society,

---

58   Ibid.
59   Ibid.
60   Ibid.

since access to land and therefore survival depends on obedience to the community. Patzi believes that there are three aspects that define the presence of a communal system:

> The market stalls of the traders are not privately owned but managed by the union, and so the owner is the collective, the sellers are possessors. Or, to put it differently, trade has the same role as land within the community—without trading one starves to death. This is one of the elements. Nobody could understand why people obey and why those who don't attend have to pay a fine. Why pay? What coercive elements are there? They can lose their market stall and if they don't have one, they risk becoming marginalized. The second element is the neighborhood council. The areas that do not yet have basic services are the most effective in mobilizing. In those areas, getting access to water, electricity, or gas is not an individual activity. These services are under collective control and pass through the neighborhood council. That is why they fight for a union card, and if you don't make the effort in your own street, there will be no sewage system or paving or whatever. If you were expelled from the rural community, you could always go elsewhere, but here in the city, you can't do that, neoliberalism doesn't work like that. The formation of cooperatives for water or light are collective actions that have saved the people in the absence of the state. These are resources that are constructed politically. The third element is education. As a result of the participation of parents in the struggle for education reform, they now have total control of their children's education. The parents' committees control their sons and daughters' access to education, and if you don't attend the march or whatever, the children will have a problem. So if you don't attend meetings, pay dues, or attend marches in the coming years, your child won't enter the school or you will have to pay a fine. This is how it works in primary and secondary school, not everywhere but in most places where there are school councils.

> Those are the main features. All the examples that I mentioned have their structure. Everything is organized. Each market has one—the market is the most communal of all, the councils control the territory. Control is col-

lective and communal in the zone, in the neighborhood, and within the union.[61]

According to Patzi, the power of the movement lies not in the organizations, or the leaders or in the level of consciousness, but in the ownership or management of these three resources (territory, trade, education), and these allow us to talk about the existence of not only communities but also of a communal system.

Meanwhile, work coordinated by Alvaro García Linera, in line with modern sociological thinking, focuses on the mobilizing structures of local councils. He argues that they are influenced by the memory of organizing experiences within agricultural unions and miners' syndicalism.[62] Although his analytical perspective is different, in the sense that he does not see the local councils as communities, he nevertheless agrees that they share characteristics with rural communities: like, for example, mediation in disputes between neighbors or sanctions imposed that involve working for the benefit of the barrio. In any case, he notes that the boards exhibit "autonomous behavior" with strong local and district leadership without the need for mediation from the senior members of the FEJUVE, demonstrating a trend towards a "horizontal kind of organizational experience."[63]

He believes that in El Alto there is a "community of neighbors" formed by the rebellion of October 2003, which was characterized—according to Weber—by "the mere fact of residential proximity."[64] But reality is not so simple in El Alto. Weber himself contrasted community with association, and argues that while the latter is based on rational agreements of self-interest, the community is a subjective relationship between those who constitute a whole.[65] He argues that the concepts of solidarity and representation are in opposition, and attributes the first to community relations and the second to associations directed toward achieving specific ends.

There is no doubt that during the insurrection of October 2003 the characteristics often attributed to the local councils appeared, but the social cohesion seems to go beyond what happens just on the big day of mobilization. In that sense, it seems necessary to understand what happens in the everyday, starting with insurrectional events but going beyond.

From a very different perspective, Rafael Indaburu's work (which we will analyze in detail later) emphasizes the form in which

---

61 Interview with Félix Patzi.
62 Alvaro García Linera, ibid., 601.
63 Ibid., 603.
64 Max Weber, ibid., 293–294.
65 Ibid., 33.

the division of lots began in the more than 400 urbanizations existing in the city today. "The problems generated during the parceling out of lots, often clandestine and in conflict with real estate speculators, has led to an intensifying spirit of solidarity among residents as buyers of defective real estate."[66] In effect, the fear of fraud, the non-recognition or non-approval of the allotments by the municipality, acted as a force that united and mobilized the neighborhood. Moreover, the local councils are not barrio-based (Indaburu argues that a barrio must have a minimum of one thousand lots, while in El Alto the average for each urbanization is less than 300 lots). In short, a mosaic of many small urbanizations, each with a small, militant grassroots organization without fixed representation separate from the base, and with enough control over its members to withstand long and hard conflicts. Because of this, "a system of local organization that is deeply connected to the grassroots of each lot and with a distinct name for each urbanization" was born.[67] And because of this, local committees in El Alto are very different from the rest of the country:

> The lists of neighbors/buyers (some with phone numbers), the allotment plans, the location of each site, the number and the owner of each lot, and a careful record of the purchase papers, the property deeds, and payment of taxes, constitute the common denominator in the formation and operation of neighborhood organizations in El Alto. Unlike La Paz, where the local organization has no access to such documentation ... [68]

It is clear that what the councils in El Alto actually do—to the horror of those who drafted the USAID report—is fulfill the functions of the state. But there is no *one* state; there is a veritable dispersion of authority (at least with respect to territorial control) in some 500 units. The *one* gives way to the *multiple*. Therefore, no representation or control of the population is possible.

The "problem," according to the USAID study, goes further and becomes "infinite." The existence of a multiplicity of units of less than one thousand residents has generated strong "group solidarity in each urbanization in the emerging struggle against the possibility of being deceived by real estate speculators" and "against bureaucratic city administration after years and years of struggle."[69] And this dispersion has the capacity to strengthen itself, not only because

---

66   Rafael Indaburu, ibid., 21
67   Ibid.
68   Ibid.
69   Ibid., 29.

it generates fragmentation, and puts obstacles in the way of developing small scale services, which can't reach enough people to justify the investment. In fact, "the possibilities of planning for social facilities have been quashed by the neighbors who, as 'owners of tax co-participation resources,' insist on the construction of schools and health centers where they are not needed."[70]

Finally, it should be noted that while we are closer to the position of Mamani and Patzi in the analysis of the local councils, insofar as we think that the neighborhood organization has a communal characteristic, it is questionable whether there is "collective ownership *and* private use" in neighborhoods of El Alto because of the reality of genuine collective ownership, as regards the three elements identified by Patzi above, as well as other variables. What doubtless do exist are social relations, relations between neighbors, in which the "we" bears a much heavier weight than the "I," as much for strictly material reasons as for symbolic and cultural ones.

However, it is worth mentioning that while individuals technically own each lot, that is in reality a mere formality. Legal uncertainty leads residents to unite and build alliances with their peers, due to the lack of services, the helplessness before crime or the municipality (the implementation of the Maya y Paya taxes provoked an uprising); basically, the complete insecurity and helplessness felt by each family unit. This unity within the community organization is the ultimate security that assures people that they will retain their lot, housing, and services—in short, their lives. Henceforth, we will see how the undivided community does not need to create separate bodies to defend itself, impart justice, meet the population's basic needs, or exercise power. This non-division exists, though not in a pure form, because it shares space-time with a division—not as something faraway and separate but, as Foucault indicates, in a relation of "complex interiority." But before discussing this, we will observe another aspect of the community: the tendency towards dispersion.

---

70 Ibid.

CHAPTER 2

The Self-Constructed City: Dispersion and Difference

A study coordinated by Rafael Indaburu for the US Agency for International Development (USAID)/Bolivia offers a synthetic but concise elite vision of the problems in El Alto and the challenges that the social movement presents to dominant sectors.[1] It is a "rapid evaluation" carried out by a group of professionals commissioned by USAID following the insurrection in October 2003 (the research and writing of the report were done between December 2003 and January 2004), with the objective of encouraging actions to head off the movements in El Alto.

Methodologically speaking, the study's "panoramic" approach to the subject is curious. It uses aerial photographs, maps, satellite images, and statistics with the aim of preparing an "intelligent plan" that articulates and separates the different variables analyzed.[2] This methodology tends to consolidate a rigid separation between the subject and object with no concessions: the "objects"—the population of El Alto—never get to speak, while the "subjects" of the investigation are limited to a small group of "key informants" who are never mentioned by name or cited directly. This methodology, whose use is by no means coincidental, leads to a set of proposals in line with the objective of the study—to destroy the social movement in El Alto and especially the grassroots organization of the neighborhood councils.

The selection of a particular methodology is always coherent with the objectives pursued. In this case, the objectives include reconfiguring the El Alto social movement by smoothing over, to say the least, its anti-systemic characteristics. This presupposes that the movement and the people in it are the objects of research and policies designed and applied in the service of the needs of neo-colonial elites, without taking into account their desires or interests.[3]

---

1 Indaburu, Rafael. "Evalacuion de la ciudad de El Alto."

2 Indaburu, ibid., 2.

3 Rivera, Silvia. "El potencial epistemológico y teórico de la historia oral: de la lógica instrumental a la descolonización de la historia" in *Temas Sociales, La*

Separation, or division, is the analytical point of departure for Indaburu's work. On the one hand, physical separation appears (La Ceja as a geographical break), added to institutional separation (municipal autonomy obtained by El Alto in 1986), concluding that "the main historic moments in El Alto are moments of affirmation of the division or separation from La Paz."[4] Based on this statement, the study moves directly to question and debate the symbolic or conceptual aspects born of any separation: difference. Difference is evaluated as the first problem to resolve and throughout the work it appears as the most negative characteristic of the population of El Alto. Indaburu also mentions "regionalist exclusivism"—judged to be a form of "racism and xenophobia"—the separation and difference between North El Alto and South El Alto, and the social and neighborhood differences that provoke "ethnic intolerance."[5]

From the urban point of view, one of the problems that emerges as a determining factor in the current situation is the existence of separate neighborhoods ("urban islands differentiated within the social fabric") that provoke "a strict separation of some urban settlements from others." Indaburu sees these islands as "internally disarticulated" since the "centralities are still very precarious."[6] Note that for him the articulating force must be a center, negating the possibility of self-articulation based on self-organization. Reflecting this premise, he proposes initiatives that point to "integration, inclusion, development, hope, and complementarity with other cities and subregions."[7] For that to occur, it is necessary to overcome the fragmentation and division in more than 400 urbanizations and to create neighborhood identities that integrate these "islands." According to the study, that would help overcome the "presently fragmented and atomized" neighborhood organizations and facilitate the implementation of a "deepening democracy and citizen responsibility."[8]

Indaburu considers the "dispersion" of the city into hundreds of lots the major problem: it provokes low density, between four and five times less than in La Paz—in a discontinuous and chaotic city that the study deems scarcely consolidated. The study attributes these characteristics to the low level of institutional development and a lack of administrative organization. He believes that the origin of the problem is the illegal and irregular way that hundreds

---

Paz, No.11; and Raúl Zibechi, "La emancipación como producción de vínculos" in *Hegemonías y Emancipaciones* (Buenos Aires: FLACSO, 2005).

4   Indaburu, ibid., 5.
5   Ibid., 6.
6   Ibid., 7.
7   Ibid., 8.
8   Ibid., 9.

of individual settlers divided the city, with no government control. This purportedly led to insecurity for buyers, who are often victims of fraud and wind up with property titles that are not accepted as collateral, thus depriving them of access to credit. Indaburu notes, "formal credit institutions do not want to accept El Alto real estate as collateral, which—if executed—is more of a headache than an asset with financial value."[9] Under these conditions, capitalism cannot prosper. But the root problem does not lie in the ownership of the land, rather in social relations based on solidarity that cause high levels of conflict in El Alto:

> The problems that the often clandestine and conflictive subdivision generated with the developers (old and new), has meant that solidarities between neighbors have deepened as buyers of defective real estate... The concerns stemming from possible fraud and the municipality's non-recognition and non-approval of these land subdivisions keep the neighbors united and aggressively mobilized to defend their investments. These conditions give rise to a system of neighborhood organization strongly articulated based on each lot and with the distinctive name of each "urbanization."[10]

This "fragmented" form of neighborhood organization is seen as an obstacle since its enormous dispersion makes state action difficult. The study urges that the over 500 urbanizations of between 300 and 1,000 residents should be articulated in barrios of five to eight thousand inhabitants, which could be considered "minimal thresholds of life in urban communities."[11] In this way two objectives of "development" would be fulfilled: the construction of urban apparatus by scale, that is, more profitability, and "citizen participation and deepening of democracy."[12]

If you strip the study of its ideological judgments (for example, drug trafficking and delinquency are placed in the same category as the grassroots struggle for the university), what you have is an analysis that looks at dispersion as the main problem for the elites to combat the popular insurgency in El Alto. The concept of dispersion appears stated in several ways: fragmentation, division, sectarianism, and even xenophobia, among others.

What is the purpose of saying that the small-scale impedes "development"? Why the necessity to articulate neighborhood groups

---

9   Ibid., 20.
10 Ibid., 21.
11 Ibid., 22.
12 Ibid., 24.

into larger units and encourage a policy that produces "centralities" in neighborhoods that are considered "disarticulated"? When the study states that "the excessive fragmentation of the neighborhood organizations makes it difficult for urban integration, what are the implications?

The entire study commissioned by USAID is tainted by the attack on dispersion because dispersion makes it hard to exert social control. It impedes the creation of an urban-political panoptic — political but also social, cultural and organizational — that could en- capsulate broad populations under the same umbrella of control. In other words, fragmentation or dispersion implies face-to-face rela- tions in the villas, articulated among the people themselves and with other urbanizations based on forms developed in everyday life. What they seek in instituting larger neighborhoods is to open up spaces to representation — meaning the absence of representatives — under the euphemism of "participation and democracy." This is the best way the capitalist system has found to control large concentrations of the population. Larger territorial units give way to massive social orga- nizations that inevitably cannot function through direct democracy based on family units. Assemblies of villas with 200 or 300 families can't operate the same way as neighborhoods that embody the re- solve of 10,000 or more inhabitants.

To comply with these objectives, the intrinsic dispersion and difference in El Alto are aspects to neutralize or better, to substitute for a process of homogenization. From there comes the emphasis on "inclusion" and "integration" — soft ways of saying that what's needed is to annul differences. Similarly, the need for institution- alization seems to be in order to achieve administrative and urban rationality, even for the social movement. "Rational" is understood exclusively as state rationality, never that of the subjects themselves, who are always considered irrational or in terms of the political left, "spontaneous."

The objective in the long term is to "deliver" the services nec- essary to the population, but to do it in such a way as to produce cultural and social homogeneity. Thus, educational and health ser- vices should be in the hands of the state but on the condition that there is a "minimal threshold" of population, to be administered by a state bureaucracy separated from the fragmented urban "islands." When the study asserts dismissively that "any group can construct a school or a health center with donated funds," they are doubting that self-managed education and health systems can exist even on a small scale. In this sense, for them the small neighborhood school or the preventive health clinic based on herbal medicines and *yat-*

iris[13] — the dispersing of these services — is an evil to be combated. Grassroots community self-management in education and health, as well as any other service or action, always goes hand-in-hand with dispersion, since centralization and concentration are state/capitalist forms. Lastly, it is worthwhile to consider that what is deemed "urban chaos," or even the much-feared "social chaos" supposes a vision from outside looking in that does not understand that this chaos is the product of the dispersing activity of the Aymara, Quechua, miners, and peasant population. The supposed chaos is the product of an outpouring from below, that's all.

Based on the above, it can be concluded that not only the economic and political elites of Bolivia and the transnational corporations have an interest in overcoming the state of dispersion that rules in the Aymara world of El Alto. The left also seems tempted to do it, since it is based on the same ideological sources that idolize progress and the "civilizing" actions of nation-states. It would not be strange if in the future the Bolivian left — even the indigenous — tried to finish a task at which the colonial elites failed.

But these are not the only forms of dispersion of the capitalist state. The tension towards dispersion, for sure, permeates throughout society. Take the example of the so-called informal sector and the family economy. In El Alto — one of the most carefully analyzed cities by the state and nongovernmental organizations — seventy percent of the employed population works in the family sector (fifty percent) or home businesses (twenty percent).[14] This occurs mostly in trade and restaurants (ninety-five percent of those employed), followed by construction (eighty percent) and manufacturing (seventy-five percent). Youth predominate in these sectors: more than half of employees in manufacturing are between twenty and thirty-five years old, with women being the overwhelming majority in trade and restaurants in the category of family and informal businesses.[15] Seventy-nine percent of women who work, do so in these sectors.

The main protagonist in the El Alto labor market is "the family, as an economic unit generating employment or the source of the greatest number of waged workers." In these spaces, a "new labor and social culture" emerges, marked by nomadism, insecurity, and different working relations. This type of employment is typically

---

13   Traditional medical practitioners and community healers among the Aymara.

14   The informal business units have at least four workers, with one or two family members, in general the owner who also works, and another two hired workers.

15   Bruno Rojas and german Guaygua, "Employment in Times of Crisis." *Avances de Investigación* #24, (La Paz: Cedla, 2003).

considered from the perspective of its weakness: it is judged as precarious, informal, backward, badly paid, and unproductive, etc. In general, it is thought of as a transitory employment and "a desperate option for survival."[16]

It is not often thought that this sector or, better said, this type of work, which is clearly expanding, has any advantages. According to several studies, in the last two decades employment in the familial and semi-business sectors has done nothing but grow. In 1989, it comprised 64.4 percent of the economically active population and in 1995 it had grown nearly by one tenth to reach 73.5 percent, the family sector grew from 53.9 percent to 56.8 percent and the semi-business went from 10.7 to 16.8 percent.[17] Another study, confirming this tendency, showed that in 1992 both sectors accounted for sixty-four percent of employment in El Alto and sixty-nine percent in 2000.[18]

This type of employment has some characteristics worth pointing out. Since there is no internal division of labor in the informal sector like there is in manufacturing, there is also no separation of the worker from the object produced, because the labor is performed communally. Also, because there are no worker-boss relationships, that place is occupied by the affective social relations between relatives and friends.[19]

A qualitative investigation of the family unit, in which half of the economically active population of El Alto works, concludes that there is no separation between the property and management of the economic unit, and the productive process. In the semi-business sector, this separation only occurs with respect to property. The division of labor in the workplace, even where the merchandise passes through different processes, is at a minimum. Besides exceptional cases, all those who work can rotate tasks without harming the productive process. In family units, unpaid family labor predominates in most of the cases studied; some teach others how to do the work, and the management of time invested in producing a product is the sole responsibility of the worker so long as he or she fulfills the orders on time.[20] The study points out that some micro-businesses encompass

16   Ibid., presentation by Javier Gómez A., Executive Director of CEDLA.

17   Pablo Rosell, *Diagnóstico socioeconómico de El Alto: distritos 5 y 6* (La Paz: CEDLA, 1999), 27.

18   Pablo Rosell and Bruno Rojas, *Destino Incierto: Esperanzas y realidades laborales de la juventud alteña* (La Paz: CEDLA, La Paz, 2002), 14.

19   Diego Palma, *La Informalidad, lo popular y el cambio social* (La Paz: ILDIS, 1988) cited by Rafael Archondo, ibid., 65.

20   Pablo Poveda, "*Trabajo, informalidad y acumulación*" Cuaderno #30 (La Paz: 2003), 22–23.

a wide group of family units and that the "owner," in addition to pay-
ing for work performed, gives the families "help" or "loans in time of
need."[21]

In these workplaces, another sociologist observes "greater
autonomy in labor management" since it is "a productive activity
that is not under the direct supervision of a boss."[22] He adds that
these forms of production are non-capitalist (although in his opinion
the market and capital "refunctionalize" them) and insists that they
are not transitory but "the historic form in the medium term of the
broader reproduction of capital in Bolivia."[23]

In conclusion, the majority of the workers in El Alto and of the
country are not subject to the Taylorist division of labor. The workers dominate the management of time in production and practice an
almost indivisible organization of labor, with the ability to rotate from
one post to another. We are looking at young, largely female workers
who are very poor and educated (there is only a eight percent illit-
eracy rate in El Alto and fifty-two percent have had at least one year
of secondary school), with great autonomy in their jobs and a strong
family presence. It was these workers who were the protagonists of
the September–October 2003 insurrection and the main battles of
this cycle of protest.

If we go beyond the "limits" attributed to family and informal
units, the popular sectors have put in place, for the first time in the
urban space, a series of self-controlled production methods, although
articulated and dependent on the market. Nevertheless, this should
not cause us to lose sight of the fundamental fact that vast sectors of
workers control the forms and time of their own productive activity
and are no longer dominated by capitalist time and its division of labor. In the first stage, the new poor concentrate on building survival
strategies in the service industries, recycling the waste of consumer
society, and taking advantage of fissures to secure a foothold in commercial areas like micro-business or family initiatives. In time, they
begin producing.

Is there a relationship between this type of labor and familial
autonomy, and the fact that these sectors have been able to stage an
insurrection without leadership or leaders? The question is relevant
because, during the period in which workers gave up the organization of the work process to the boss and the management of society
to the state, struggle required the use of centralized, hierarchical
structures and dependence on the labor and political leaders that

---

21   Ibid., 17.

22   Alvaro García Linera, *Reproletarización. Nueva calse obrera y desarrollo del capital industrial en Bolivia (1952-1998)* (La Paz: Muela del Diablo, 1999), 118.

23   Ibid., 201.

represented them and made the decisions. And, on the other hand, a larger question arises: what is the relationship between capital and the state's inability to exercise micro-control (over the family, school, and work) and the growing militarization of our societies?

These are not idle questions. Silvia Rivera, while pointing out that we should acknowledge the positive aspects of relations of self-employment, reminds us that in the popular indigenous urban sectors of Bolivia "politics is not defined so much in the streets as in the most intimate environment of the markets and domestic units, classic arenas of female action."[24] The series of characteristics that we have attributed to the privileged role of the family in anti-systemic movements goes hand in hand with a reconfiguration of political spaces as a whole and also, therefore, the forms it adopts, the channels through which it transmits itself, and even the relationship between means and ends that it seeks. Identifying exactly how female leadership and the centrality of domestic units[25] changes the content of politics and methods of social change remains a question for further research.

In any case, to think that the popular and indigenous sectors "fall" into the informal and familial economy out of "desperation" presupposes that they are objects and not the subjects of their own lives. Wallerstein notes that they make a choice, as a community, to perpetuate themselves as an ethnic group and to survive in a period of intense aggression at the hands of the elite. In addition to asserting that domestic units are one of the pillars of the world system (on the same level of importance as state, class, or business), Wallerstein points out that "normally all members of the domestic unit share the same ethnicity."[26] In this case, the urban Aymara and other poor socialize in domestic units in which they not only work and survive but that also "constitute the main agent of socialization in the norms of the ethnicity," that is, in cultural norms that differentiate them from others.[27]

In other words, without the family and semi-business economy, Aymara who emigrate to the city would fall (here this term makes sense) into working for big, private businesses or government apparatuses. Many would consider that a "privilege," but it would occur at the cost of the destruction of their own culture. If the Ay-

---

24   Silvia Rivera, *Bircholas* (La Paz: Mama Huaco, 1996), 132.

25   Wallerstein defines a domestic unit as "a unit that unites in a common space the income of its members to assure its maintenance and reproduction," in "Las unidades domesticas como instituciones de la economia-mundo." *Capitalismo historico y movimientos antisistemicos* (Madrid: Akal, 2004), 235.

26   Ibid., 239.

27   Ibid., 238.

mara of the Altiplano continue to be Aymara—human beings different from others—it is because they chose to socialize in affinity-based relationships with relatives and comrades, in which Western anthropologists and sociologists see only exploitation and accumulation. In the Aymara culture—in a different way in the cities than the countryside—mechanisms of compensation for these inequalities seems to have been created.

CHAPTER 3

Everyday Life and Insurrection: Undivided Bodies

The descriptions that we have of the October uprising make it clear that no body separate from the neighborhood communities was formed to lead or give content to the movement. Not only did it sidestep the leaders and neighborhood councils, the unions, and any another formal organization, but the uprising was "directed" by and arose from everyday forms of life. The struggle "lacked an organizer and leader" and "was executed directly by the inhabitants of the barrio and street." It also did not have a collective leadership arising from the neighborhood councils, but rather "another type of loyalty," operating on a microlevel, that "went over and, in some cases, around the margins of the authority of their own neighborhood council."[1]

Accounts of the uprising all address three aspects of the events: collective decision making at each step, the rotation of leaders and tasks, and the outpouring from below. Here the first aspect is highlighted: "On the morning of Sunday, October 12, after the massacre that occurred during the brutal clash on the afternoon of the day before, El Alto inhabitants held assemblies and meetings to decide the 'hows' of continuing the struggle."[2] Similarly, another description emphasizing collective decision making indicates that "a type of collective, rotating, and decentralized leadership has been formed."[3]

From a perspective that seeks to link territorial and micro relationships, sociologist Pablo Mamani maintains that the people seized their barrios in order "to maintain control and their own self-organization." It was "an intense mobilization that articulated collective strategies, emotions, and dignity manifest in actions coordinated by turn within families, zones, and districts as well as diverse organizations within the urban territory."[4] Thus, tasks like digging trenches and keeping watch to stop the army from entering the neighbor-

---

1 Alvaro García Linera, 2004, *Sociología de los movimientos sociales en Bolivia*, ibid., 606.
2 Luis A. Gómez, *El Alto de pie*, 89.
3 Alvaro García Linera, 54.
4 Pablo Mamani, *El rugir de las multitudes* (El Alto: Yachaywasi, 2004), 144.

hoods were carried out "by turns, zone by zone, block by block."[5] In the urban and rural bases of the uprisings, Félix Patzi maintains that a "communal ethos" had replaced the "union ethos" during the preceding five years. He points out that during the El Alto insurrection "the organizing capacity of the inhabitants was guided by communal logic at every moment." The assemblies organized by zone and by street replaced the authority of representation, and in many cases these assemblies "revitalized the neighbors council leadership, made up of militants from the Movimiento de la Izquierda Revolucionaria (MIR) and the Nueva Fuerza Republicana (NFR),[6] or obliged the parties to subordinate themselves unconditionally to the assembly."[7]

The massiveness of the Aymara mobilization—which had managed to mobilize a half-million people for several weeks in September–October of 2000—lies in the practice of taking turns, the sense of obligation, and the communal assemblies that "are revitalized in urban spaces, and lead to the massive participation of men and women."[8] But the communal ethos of the revolt goes further, given that what is emerging is another society: the objective is power, not state power, but for people to organize themselves as powers in a different social context. And far from the spaces of state control and the gaze of the media and the elites, the insurrectionaries strategize in their self-controlled spaces: "In the evening hours they devised multiple strategies. They schemed of flooding the cities with indigenous in the future by having eight to twelve children like their grandfathers, to cause the gradual disappearance of the whites, in a kind of passive war—or more actively, they thought of assaulting the military institutions and arming themselves."[9] The people were discreetly capable of accumulating large quantities of potato starch and quinoa to feed those manning the blockades—even when the flow of produce between the countryside and the city had been disrupted. Evidently, the uprising took on forms that were very different from those prevailing in institutional social and political organizations, where nothing can be done without the initiative of the leaders.

• • • • • • • • • • • • •

---

5   Ibid., 150.

6   Translator's note: The Revolutionary Left Movement and the New Republican Force.

7   Félix Patzi, "Rebelión indígena contra la colonialidad y la transnacionalización de la economía: triunfos y vicisitudes del movimiento indígena desde 2000 a 2003," in Forrest Hylton et al *Ya es otro tiempo el presente. Cuatro momentos de insurgencia indígena* (La Paz: Muela del Diablo, 2003), 261.

8   Ibid.

9   Ibid., 263.

The usual form assumed by Latin American social movements presupposes the creation of organizational bodies that are separate from the groups they represent and assume the state form. For over a century, anti-systemic movements have developed their organizational structures in parallel to capital, the state, the military, and other institutions of the system they fight. Although there are a great variety of working-class, popular, and peasant "organizations" arising out of and reflecting the vicissitudes of daily life, the political left and social movements chose to build structures that are separate. In doing so, they show not only that they have little use for the forms and structures of the everyday life of the oppressed in their effort to make a revolution and change the world, but they also—a paradox of social struggle—replace them with structures that are modeled on those of the oppressors.

These state powers present in the left and social movements seem to have two sources that ultimately spring from the same genealogy: the military machine of the state apparatus and the Taylorist organization of work. Both share the creation of a centralized and unified body separate from everyday life in order to lead society, impose homogeneity from outside, and shape it according to the wishes of those who occupy the space above. Lenin anticipated Taylorism in *What Is To Be Done?*, proposing the construction of a partisan political apparatus based on the centralized state, to which he added a division of labor between leaders and led, intellectual and manual workers, and the specialization of functions:

> Lack of specialization is one of the most serious defects of our technique .... The smaller each separate "operation" in our common cause the more people we can find capable of carrying out such operations .... On the other hand, in order to unite all these tiny fractions into one whole, in order not to break up the movement while breaking up its functions, and in order to imbue the people who carry out the minute functions with the conviction that their work is necessary and important, without which conviction they will never do the work, it is necessary to have a strong organization of tried revolutionaries.[10]

During the period of the Third International and the International Red Syndicate (IRS), the symmetry with state organization went further still. The secretary general of the IRS said: "It is possible and necessary to use the knowledge acquired in the mili-

---

10 V. I. Lenin, *What Is to Be Done?*, *Obras Completas, Tomo V* (Madrid: Akal, 1976), 476–477.

tary field for the purposes of directing strike actions."[11] The revolutionary leadership was the "General Staff" of the revolution, the workers in struggle a "striking army," and strikes forms of "combat"; the base groups were "support points for the struggle." The material resources of the union were their "ammunitions" and sympathizers made up the "rear-guard." Forms of action were established that not only used militaristic language but also, in their symmetry to the state, introduced hierarchical forms of action: the "elemental" form of struggle like an economic strike would give way to "higher stages" such as the political strike that would then lead to "the highest form of action," the insurgency. In this rationalistic and instrumental notion, the central concepts are organization, leadership, and planning, which they believed would resolve the problems posed by revolutionary struggle.

What we found in the Aymara world, both rural and urban, during the insurrection, were non-state powers. In these movements, the organization is not separate from everyday life; daily life is deployed as an arena for insurrectionary action. The division of labor is minimal because there is no separation between those who give orders and those who receive them, nor between those who think and those who do, because collective meetings fulfill these functions. The leader has no power and when exercising his or her function, is in a position "whose only institutional weapon is his or her reputation, whose only means is persuasion, and whose only rule is to oversee the wishes of the group: the leader looks more like a movie star than a man of power, and always runs the risk of being repudiated and abandoned by his own people."[12] This is how Clastres describes primitive societies in which the leader has no power,[13] so different from the "men of state" of institutional politics.

But among the Aymara are there leaders without power, bosses who are not statesmen? This description of a leader who is *not* applies perfectly to a leader such as Felipe Quispe, and many other Aymara leaders, but not to a man like Evo Morales. Morales does have power and likes to exercise it: he single-handedly decided to be the representative of the social movement. He himself decided to be a candidate for the presidency of Bolivia and to partake in government, and he leads a political body (Movement Toward Socialism, MAS in its Spanish acronym) that is separate from society in movement.

On the contrary, we speak of state power when leaders become part of the organs of power. "Special institutions are needed,

---

11   Drizdo Lossovsky, *De la huelga a la toma del poder. Los combates económicos y nuestra táctica* (Montevideo: Conferencia Sindical Latinoamericana, 1930), 3.

12   Pierre Clastres, cited by Gilles Deleuze, *Mil mesetas*, 365.

13   Pierre Clastres, *Investigaciones en antropología política*, ibid.

then, for that leader to become a statesman, but widespread collective mechanisms are needed to prevent it."[14] According to Clastres, war is that mechanism in primitive societies, because they are societies "against the state" in which "the dispersion machine works against the unification machine."[15] In Aymara society and in El Alto, the collective approach to decision making is the mechanism that prevents the formation of separate bodies, and the rotation of representatives and the outpouring from below that goes beyond institutions, the state, and even the social movement. While the first two are common in rural indigenous movements—and re-created in urban areas—the third is a novel addition, linked to population density in the space where the new movement is now located: the Aymara city of El Alto, the first major Indian city on the continent. It is the first time in Andino history that a large city can be considered—because of its hegemonic culture, the manner of its construction, and the type of social relations that prevail within it—an Aymara city.

We are looking at urban and rural societies—in parallel to the dominant society but without a doubt also connected with it—where leadership and power are separated. Power rests in the collective, in the community assembly or neighborhood council; leadership can be embodied by the representatives, the heads of the councils, or unions, including the Federation of Neighborhood Councils (FE-JUVE) or the Regional Workers Center (COR) or the local neighborhood councils.

The separation between leadership and power was clearly visible during the insurrection, when—as at decisive moments in the life of a society—power is exercised directly and, as García Linera points out, "over" or "to the side" of the authority of the neighborhood council.[16] The fact is that in this type of society the group, the urbanization, neighborhood, and community "is both complete and united."[17] This feature is not so clearly visible in everyday life, because each urban member of the Aymara group is working and embedded in the capitalist market, which atomizes people, reduces them to commodities (in the labor market) thus striping the community of its character. But if we take a broader perspective, we see that Clastres' description of primitive society—based on the mode of domestic production—is more akin to the Aymara reality than what Lenin described in *What Is to Be Done?*

---

14   Gilles Deleuze, 364.

15   Pierre Clastres, *Arqueología de la violencia: la guerra en las sociedades primitivas* (Buenos Aires, FCE, 2004), 79.

16   See *Sociología de los movimientos sociales en Bolivia*.

17   Pierre Clastres, *Arqueología de la violencia: la guerra en las sociedades primitivas*, 49.

Outside of that derived from the sexes, in primitive society there is no division of labor whatsoever: each individual is versatile in a sense, all men know everything
that men should know, all women know all the tasks a
woman must do. In the realm of knowledge, and know-
how, there is no individual that falls behind the others,
no matter how skilled or talented these might be.[18]

The Community War

The strength of Aymara non-division allowed the residents of El Alto
to defeat the machinery of the military state, which contradicts the
rational logic that holds that a body is more efficient when divided.
Because, in addition to numerical superiority, there is the virtue of
versatility. Two bodies confront each other: there is one that is specialized and whose parts can only perform one function and there is
another that is undivided, whose parts can perform all the functions.
Thus, the latter is not dependent on each single part but operates as a
complete machine, and even the amputation of one portion does not
preclude further action. In this sense, the state, army, and political
party, functioning as a chain-link hierarchy, collapse when one of
them stops working, as happens in the Fordist assembly line.

Beginning on Saturday, October 11, 2003, "a huge neighborhood force spilled out into the streets" building barricades, vigils,
bonfires, and digging deep trenches, "a force that despite being confined to their territory, exceeded these limits and *included anyone who
wished to join* the demonstrations." This social force created committees and networks of committees and special commissions, "some in
charge of the food supply for the area and collaborating with others,
and *they also made preparations for defense*. Others were responsible for
digging and maintaining the trenches and barricades."[19] Note that
underlying the whole insurrectionary movement there is a non-divided "organization" that provides supplies and coordinates defense,
laying the foundation for survival and military action. To sum up, it
is a single body, one organism, that creates units to perform all the
various functions necessary for its own survival.

Not only is there no organizational division—only different functions performed by the same social body—but the division
between leaders and led evaporates. A witness points out that "on
a voluntary basis, the neighbors ... created the framework for the

---

18   Ibid., 47.
19   Alvaro García Linera, *Sociología de los movimientos sociales en Bolivia*, 607–608,
my emphasis.

struggle."[20] If the neighborhood councils were overstepped, it is because they were more used to organizing marches and strikes—the
type of activities planned by a small core of leaders joined by a con-
siderable part of the inhabitants. This is what is usually understood
as a social movement. What happened in October was that "a sea of
people" based on "forms of intra-neighborhood cooperation" improvised new methods and forms of struggle "that exceeded previous
forms of authority and social organization."[21]

The image of "a sea" of citizens is appropriate because people
acted as a multiplicity and not in a one-directional form. Not only
were they many, but they also came from everywhere. They did not
just form one huge column, which could have been easily suppressed;
they were like water that comes in waves and surges, crashes down,
and adapts to the terrain, appearing in the most unlikely places: im-
placable, obstinate, and incomprehensible.

On the 13th and 14th, for example, the panorama was one of
El Alto occupied by the inhabitants, who kept watch and held blockades street by street, block by block. Meanwhile, thousands arrived
in La Paz and El Alto from numerous Altiplano communities—some
by main roads, in vehicles, or on foot; others by back roads or on
horseback, through the fields and over the mountains. The rebellion spread to the country's main cities and rural areas, which in
turn blocked highways and mobilized in different directions. In La
Paz, El Alto residents came down not only on the highway but also
via the surrounding streets; the inhabitants of the hillside descended
along dozens of routes to the center. And, surprisingly, from "below," the people of Ovejuyo and Chasquipampa communities on
the slopes of Illimani came and entered the city through the upper-
middle class and white neighborhoods. Furthermore, a section of
the middle classes was mobilized by means of mass hunger strikes
in the churches.[22]

A sea, a tide, flooded the survival capability of the government.
It is no coincidence that the words used to describe these days were
"waves," "ant-like," and "spilling over," etc. It is not just a question of
magnitude, but of ways: the simultaneity of multiple actions is what
allows us to speak of multiplicity. The issue is not just the 400,000
people who converged in Plaza San Francisco, La Paz on June 14,
but also how they did it. There was no *one* call from a formal institution but *many* calls—some formal but most informal, from below,
and based on the previous experiences of the workers and neighbors
who had taken over the public sphere dozens of times. Moreover,

---

20 Ibid., 608.

21 Ibid., 609.

22 Luis Gómez, *El Alto de pie*.

during the march itself down from El Alto, "many groups changed direction"[23] upon hearing the latest news—following their own internal dynamic, immanent, not guided or directed from outside but coordinated as if moving with the surroundings.

Although the days of September–October 2003—culminating with the fall of Gonzalo Sánchez de Lozada—were compared with the heroic exploits of Tupac Katari, and particularly the siege of La Paz, it seems clear that the internal dynamics of both processes were quite unique and perhaps these differences help explain the contradictory results that were achieved. In 2003, and in all major struggles since at least the year 2000, the rebels failed to act in a way that was harmonious with the state. We suggest that this is one of the reasons for the successes attained so far.

The Micro View

On the other hand, it is clear that before the magnitude of the September–October events, institutionalized forms of social action had not succeeded in curbing the sale of gas. To be on top of the events, the neighbors had to create and invent something new, and to do so they had to go out into the streets en masse, dig themselves into their barrios, and overstep the very types of social action that they had executed in the decades before. These days the El Alto community spreads out over the territory, neutralizing the armed repression by seizing areas that the army needs to pass through in order to deploy. The El Alto social machine was able to disperse the state's military machine, and to do so had to overstep their own organizations and leaders not only because they were ineffective at defending and fighting, but also because these leaders and organizations had already formed part of that "other" that needed to be dispersed, as we shall see further on.

But how does this dispersal or inhibitory machine work? And how, if it does work, does it work in everyday life? Here are some examples. First of all, there are the "tactics" invented and used by the movement to defend and attack: *pulga, sikititi, taraxchi,* and *wayronko* are among the most prevalent. To summarize: the *pulga* [flea] is a tactic utilized to block roads and streets at night, quickly, and to withdraw instantly—similar to a flea bite—and occurs simultaneously at thousands of different locations.[24] The *wayronko* [ground beetle] tactic consisted of "lightning marches and blockades to distract the

---

23   Ibid., 141.

24   Felipe Quispe, *"La lucha de los ayllus kataristas hoy."* in *Movimiento indio en América Latina: resistencia y proyecto alternativo* (México: Benemérita Universidad Autónoma de Puebla, 2005), 73–74.

forces of repression," without a route or prior plan, like the flight of the beetle, which seems to lack any predictable direction.[25] In the *sikititi* [red ant] tactic, the communities march "in line."[26] Finally, the *taraxchi* [plumed bird] tactic is a massive mobilization intended to shut down the cities.[27]

All of these action plans are rhizomatic in character, just like the lives of the animals upon which the tactics are based.[28] In effect, these plans have no centralized control, and are not carried out with any kind of command structure, since the implementation of these tactics depends on the communities and the mandatory system of rotation deployed with planned actions. These tactics, of which only the *pulga* was widely implemented, were activated after the organizations decided to blockade streets, and after extensive consultations with the communities and agricultural unions. When the blockades started, "everyone mobilized, because we are in our communities and know the strategic locations and can easily beat the enemy."[29] Communal brigades oversee the plans or, to put it differently, communards organized into groups for each specific task. The whole community participates, making and executing decisions. It is the *"ayllu* militarized": the "community structures beginning to prepare for confrontation."[30]

It should be noted that the road blockades constructed by rural farmers materialize in a different way than traditional workers' barricades. While these are more or less compact fortifications, in which demonstrators are ensconced to defend themselves (military-style), rural blockades are like a carpet of stones spread over 500 meters along the road. This means that there is no *one* place to defend but a large extended area, which does not require the presence of people to be effective. The *campesinos* are dispersed in the surrounding hills from which, based on their territorial advantage, they can harass the state's forces, making it difficult for them to advance as a result of

---

25   Gómez, *El Alto de pie*, 70.

26   Alvaro García Linera, *Sociología de los movimientos sociales en Bolivia*, 157.

27   Felipe Quispe, *"La lucha de los ayllus kataristas hoy,"* 74.

28   Different from a centralized system like the tree/root binary system, the rhizome or the *raicilla* system is multiple, heterogeneous, and its bodies undifferentiated. For Deleuze and Guattari, the rhizome "is acentric, non-hierarchical, and non-significant, without General, without organized memory or central automaton, defined solely by a circulation of states." It does not conform to external or transcendent ends, but "in a plan of immanence" and acts "by variation, expansion, conquest, capture, injection." Gilles Deleuze and Félix Guattari, *Mil mesetas* (Valencia: Pre-Textos, 1994), 26.

29   Felipe Quispe, *"La lucha de los ayllus kataristas hoy."* ibid., 74.

30   Alvaro García Linera, *Sociología de los movimientos sociales en Bolivia*, 158.

their inability to concentrate their forces on one point of resistance. At barricades, the human presence is crucial to their effectiveness, because otherwise the enemy will take them easily, but the tapestry of stones itself delays and impedes the forces of repression. Meanwhile, as the security forces are held up, rebels move to make another stone barricade further up the road, wearing down their opponents. Sometimes barricades are constructed to form part of the road blockade, as one more component of the tapestry of stone.

The system of taking turns—which ensures that the entire community or neighborhood is involved—allows the action to be maintained indefinitely. This system does not require specialized bodies that are separate from the group, like other forms of collective action such as assemblies, supplies, *aptapis* [communal meals], or sanctions, but are part of the same group assuming different tasks or taking on different roles. This is precisely what characterizes a rhizome. As forms of action that are part of everyday life of the community, employed for production or in the daily routine, the action plans do not require the creation of a special or separate structure or even specialization or division of labor. Everyone already knows what to do and what is expected from each person and, above all, from each family.

This can be formulated differently: the system of rotation, the assemblies, and the other forms of action are community social relations, of labor and organization, deployed in rural and urban areas. These are non-capitalist, non-centralized, and self-articulated relations. This "other" society that is set in motion also has other relationships and other ways of organizing itself.

The logic of dispersal means that there is no single, prioritized form of social action, but a wide range that is activated in a decentralized and natural manner, without waiting for orders from a nonexistent central command. A good example is that of unplanned street blockades outside of the neighborhood, based on forms or traditions of everyday life. This happened in the strike in March 2001, when "women created a blockade by sitting down in the middle of the avenues, chewing coca and chatting in Aymara or Spanish." By doing so, they made the main streets and junctions "a sort of group assembly where even the children are involved."[31] The same tendency to organize by streets and blocks, the use of hundreds of bicycles to communicate between barrios and districts, as well as flooding radio shows with calls so that the message or call to action goes out over the air, show the existence of not just one single channel of communication (top down)—as happens in traditional organizations—but

---

31   Pablo Mamani, *Los microgobiernos barriales en el levantamiento de la ciudad de El Alto* (El Alto, 2004, unpublished), 21.

a multiplicity of channels and forms of intercommunication and action.

Something similar happens with the Aymara barracks, both in the Altiplano and those that appeared in the El Alto neighborhoods during the insurrectionary days of October 2003. These barracks have nothing in common with the kind of barracks occupied by the army: they are not even clearly demarcated physical and fortified spaces. The district barracks of El Alto, as they appeared in October in District 5, were characterized as "a command headquarters for the entire area and the barrios were free to organize their own troops and their own plans of attack and defense."[32] This brief description reveals the absence of a centralizing spirit, since the barrios were entitled to determine their own plans. The geography of the Tupac Katari barrio was divided into two parts, like the two *parcialidades* of the rural *ayllus* ("in A and B to patrol the streets") — one zone being responsible for supplies and the other for defense. Meanwhile in Villa Ingenio, traditional authorities (*mallkus*) were elected to command the actions. In Huayna Potosi, they planned the takeover of the district police barracks.[33] In sum, each barrio was free to do what it considered most appropriate under the circumstances, indicating that there was no unified plan laid out centrally. At best, many initiatives converged in one plan of immanence.

So, what are we talking about when we say "barracks"? They are social relationships: organizational forms based on collective decision making and the obligatory rotation of duty, but in a militarized state or, in other words, adapted to cope with violent assault. While function and structure, and the type of tasks undertaken are different, the organization remains the same because it is always constituted by community ties.[34] In response to an emergency situation, work and action groups are formed to execute different and diverse tasks; they are not permanent bodies but created for just those actions. They are transitional arrangements for an armed/military action in a given area. This means commanders, who are also transient, and spe-

---

32   Luis Gómez, *El Alto de pie*, 84.

33   Ibid., 84–85.

34   Maturana and Varela distinguish "organization" from "structure:" a system characterized by organization is the set of relationships among its components; while the structure of the system is the physical manifestation of the organization. A type of self-managed organization which is a living system in which the product of its operations is its own organization. (Alberto Maturana and Francisco Varela, *Machines and Living Things* (Santiago: Universitaria, 1995). In the case we are looking at, we can say that the organization of Aymara society is the community, while the structures are neighborhood committees, peasant federations, barracks, etc.

cialized groups break down the foot bridges on the major avenues, groups which are linked to a specific activity and then later disperse back into everyday life relations. Even larger "military" actions like the derailment of train cars in La Ceja to block the highways were basically community actions, involving entire families.

The experience of the Qalachaka barracks can be taken as a reference point for the kind of relations established during the moments of militarization. Near the town of Achacachi, a short distance from the school/*ayllu* of Warisata and Lake Titicaca, there is the Aymara headquarters. Those who visit will find a hill of medium height with a rocky summit and nothing else. A barracks? An abandoned hill? They will insist that the barracks are there and there is no question of doubting that. The barracks—or, better to say, the communities in a state of militarization—appear and disappear, they are discontinuous in terms of formal logic. The continuities are elsewhere: they are the rural and urban communities, which are expressed in different ways depending on the moment. They are *ayni* (mutual aid) in work; they are rotation in the duties of the authorities; they are the collective decisions of the assemblies; there are many other things ... and they are barracks during the uprisings. There is no separation or organization separate from everyday life. The same "organization" that oversees daily work or the fiesta, also oversees the street mobilization and the armed uprising.

A member of the Qalachaka barracks explained the training process:

> We would found our own barracks and say to ourselves... if we agree that we are to be our own government, we need to have our own community armed force. It was founded emotionally. That's why we created it. It was our brothers who are leaders ... and the base was totally convinced that for governing it should have these two parts. The indigenous soldiers must have preparation, they must be not just soldiers, but they should also be supervisors, like a professor with a gun.[35]

Asked about the differences between the Indian army and the Bolivian army, he had no hesitation: "The Indian army is commanded by the assemblies, it is an *ayllu* army. The *ayllu* directs the army. . . It is a democratic army, managed by the *ayllu*." As for the "officials," he said that there is no division between those who give the orders and those who fight because "in the Indian army one is a commander because of one's merit and not for eternity; others may be more capable.

---

35 Interview with Juan Carlos Condori.

That is, it is rotating, cyclical, using the same system of rotation as the *ayllu*. Everyone has an equal chance to be commander."[36]

Note that even in a militarized social relation, the "supreme command" is always the community assembly and rotation is the norm—a form of participation that prevents separate structures from binding. From this account, it appears that the barracks are not a physical space but a set of social relations that are embodied in know-how, a memory that is activated when there is a real threat or a community decision to fight militaristically. That explains why barracks do not physically exist but are a relationship, a power/capacity that can be activated in moments of conflict:

> At this moment there are no physical barracks, but I think there are about ten … that can reappear at any time during the mobilizations. There everyone is a soldier. In the mobilizations, we declare a state of war. We are at war, so everyone is a soldier, we are all one. It is not only those of the Indian army that must learn to handle weapons, but everyone—so everybody takes up arms, even the children. We do not want only one to be the chief; we can't have that. There can't be concentrated power, because that's capitalism.[37]

The same community logic applies when it is time to choose the "leaders." During moments of militarization, a differentiation is made between leaders and "commanders." "We consider those chosen by the *ayllu* to be commanders. But then the leaders go to a secondary position, and those who occupy the first position are the operatives. The executives go to second place." The community intends to create an environment in which "everyone can be *mallkus*, not only those who are the most qualified," because "they can always buy off the best, but if everyone is prepared.…"[38]

In this area, the community continues to function as a dispersal machine, always avoiding the concentration of power, and by allowing everyone to be a leader or commander, it inhibits the emergence of leaders with power over the long term. In short, we see a set of mechanisms in play that strengthen non-division by preventing any single apparatus from becoming detached from the community framework. These mechanisms also inhibit the formation of a permanent leadership by means of the rotation system. We can speak then of how the Aymara have established "war machines"—that are dispersion machines, both outwardly and inwardly, because they

---

36 Ibid.
37 Ibid.
38 Ibid.

combat the state and break it up but without creating a centralized or unified apparatus to replace it. Or, we could say, they disperse the state without re-creating it. That is precisely why they can disperse it. Simply put: the way to disperse the state is by not creating a state.

These social relationships are also visible in the way that El Alto residents have constructed their urban space. It is different from other cities: the amalgamation of self-constructed neighborhoods, distinct from one another, means that there are no long, linear streets within the neighborhoods that serve as panopticons. Outside the major avenues—the entry and exit roads to La Paz—the panorama is one of a labyrinthine network of neighborhoods with an infinity of dead-end streets, twisting and turning on invisible or nonexistent axes. Districts often do not have commercial centers, only communications nodes at the junctions of major roads:

> The municipality does not plan the layout. A group of neighbors comes together, and settles or buys and builds its own streets, so there is no continuity. There is no visible continuity. The presence of the state is not visible in the streets nor was it involved in the urban plan. But what the inhabitants have done is very strategic. In October [the military] went into the north, where the streets are open, but then they could not find the way out. For urban Aymaras, El Alto is familiar territory. Unintentionally, without planning it, this has become very useful. But there is an order, it has its plazas, its directionality, its entry and exit routes in every neighborhood. It is not capricious; there are avenues that lead from one side to the other and come together in La Ceja. For a Spanish or French architect it would seem like absolute chaos and disorder and they wouldn't understand why we would live in a city so architecturally disorganized. Sometimes it is difficult to leave the barrio and the people ask for directions and the locals help them. It is a very friendly place because sometimes it is easy to be lost. This is how you manage the urban cartography.[39]

Barrio life revolves around the plazas and the soccer fields, which consolidate community relations and become the spaces where these relationships are expressed and take shape. In general, they are the first spaces to be built by residents collectively, and disputes over the ownership of these spaces has been a source of intense conflict that shapes the "us" of the barrio/community, separating the inhab-

---

39   Interview with Pablo Mamani Ramirez.

itants and their neighborhood council from the "others." "The first thing the residents build when they arrive in a neighborhood is the sports field. It is a defining axis."[40] Public spaces serve not only to provide a sense of belonging to a place for the people who built them, but are also periodically re-appropriated during the fiestas, for sport or meetings of the local councils.

The plazas played an important role in the concentration and non-division of social action during October days. "Formal decisions were made in the plaza, and ritual acts performed in the church."[41] This is a product of a different kind of urban area, non-state in both its construction and conception. The plazas have their own histories in the urban social struggles in Bolivia, as privileged spaces for exchange among popular sectors. So, it comes as no surprise that during the October events they were the place where residents, acting as a community, made the most important decisions. The plazas acted as nodes for community consolidation and interconnection, within each neighborhood and among neighborhoods and districts:

> The plaza is the most important. It is the central point for convening residents. The soccer field is in the plaza, the place for socializing, as is the parish church, and that is where you will find the neighbors. The plaza is the space for holding neighborhood meetings. The plaza becomes everyone's large backyard; in the Andean community, one cannot have a house without a backyard. Here in El Alto there are plenty of tired little backyards, but the plaza is the big patio. Everything is done there, from lectures to meetings. But mostly the plazas are for meeting people, at a sporting event, or a party, the anniversary of the zone, a political campaign. The plaza is a large backyard, a backyard for all.

The big backyard means a lot for the people; each neighborhood has its own plaza. It is inconceivable that you wouldn't have one. If not, you have to take over the street, close it off, and there you have one. The plaza is key. Now the plaza is also an extension of the house, and in that sense is an intimate place. If you have heard some news story and you want to go somewhere immediately where you can chat about this story, and where you will find your pal, your friend, your buddies, then it is the plaza, the soccer field, the church because you never tell your dad that you are going to the plaza, you say I'm off to the library, to the church, and that means the plaza,

---

40   Interview with Marco Quispe.

41   Pablo Mamani, *Los microgobiernos barriales en el levantamiento de la ciudad de El Alto*, 46.

socializing, parties, the place to bring parties to an end. Fiestas begin in other zones and travel though them and enter the plaza and finish there, to make it more visible, to show that the party has occurred. The market is there, the fairground is there.[42]

To summarize this process: the neighborhood communities first take shape in the mass assemblies in the plazas; then after making decisions, the assemblies disperse into a multitude of actions (blockades, communication between neighborhoods and districts, marches, vigils, solidarity commissions, support for other zones, campfires, *aptapis* [communal meals], digging ditches, etc.). Thirdly, another mass concentration takes place (the march to La Ceja or La Paz). To be exact, it should be said that first of all there is a massive sovereign assembly; secondly, a series of multiple actions in the community, deployed in parallel; and thirdly, a regrouping, or rather a confluence, but of a much larger scale than the original.

As to the forms of action, we see mass meetings, assemblies, and communal meals, huge community events; then we see the moment of dispersion, that of the "flea bite"; and lastly the "final" mass action, putting into play an enormous, blunt force. It seems like a game of concentration/dispersion. The moment of concentration initially seeks to garner internal strength in the form of consensus. It is not a matter of external concentration, in the form of mass or multitude, but an internal form of concentration, more spiritual than material, since there is no single gathering, but many in various neighborhood communities.

After combat, they disperse, and this is where the effectiveness of dispersion can be seen, as a disarticulation of the repressive state apparatus. Finally there is another movement of concentration but now it is mobile, in movements and marches starting in a variety of places, not necessarily in the communities but also in the spaces from where the state was dispersed, the hundreds of nodes of blockades, assemblies, combat zones. They form a multiplicity of streams that converge in this space that the *long memory* has fixed as the place for the final confrontation or, one could say, of the concentration-in-movement: the Plaza de San Francisco, the space where the popular sectors challenge and clash with the plaza of power, la Murillo.

Communication in Movement

Bolivian social movements have a long tradition of having their own communications media, at least since the period when the miners' radio stations played their important role in trade union struggles and in the reproduction of the miner's identity. More recently, radio

---

42   Interview with Marco Quispe.

has played a significant part in the establishment of new rural and urban subjects.[43] The second generation of radio stations linked to the movement emerged in 1982, around the time that democracy was restored. The CSUTCB[44] understood at that time that radio "had played a prominent role in the organization process and unity of the people" and that it was "an instrument that helped us unify the *campesino* movement and, from that came CSUTCB."[45] The organization found that communication "must be a community creation."

In the 1990s, the Erbol (Radio Education of Bolivia) network defined popular communication as "a practice oriented towards social change" and, at a meeting held in 1995, decided to focus on communication "as a relation, recognizing that people are social beings, and that we are in constant interaction."[46] Relations between radio and communities are close. In the first stage, radio facilitated relations between the communities and state institutions, then later boosted the Aymara community culture, and over the years came to form part of community life. Since 1986, the experience of the "popular reporters" in the province of La Paz has been vital in shaping a generation of community journalists. Some incidents reveal the depth of the ties between radios and communities: in 1983, at the request of people of the Wila Sacos communities, Radio Omasuyos Andino was born in Achacachi: "the equipment was built with spare parts and accessories from old televisions, old record players, and big old radios that were no longer used."[47]

In the events of September–October 2003, radios were part of the internal communication network of the El Alto social movement, most notably Radio San Gabriel,[48] which transmitted and covered the hunger strike by hundreds of Aymara leaders (*jilakatas* and

---

43   One of the most recent works on the subject is that of Gennaro Condori Laruta, *"Experiencias comunicacionales de la Asociación de Radioemisoras Aymaras de La Paz"* in Esteban Ticona (comp.) *Los Andes desde los Andes* (La Paz: Yachaywasi, 2003).

44   Unique Confederation of Rural Laborers of Bolivia.

45   Intervention by Jaime Apaza of the CSUTCB in *"Taller Andino de Intercambio de Experiencias en Educación y Comunicación de Organizaciones Campesino-Indúenas"* (Ecuarunari, Quito, 1989), 114.

46   Erbol, *"Estrategia de comunicación alternativa para el desarrollo,"* (La Paz: 1995), 13.

47   Gennaro Condori Laruta, *"Experiencias comunicacionales de la Asociación de Radioemisoras Aymaras de La Paz,"* op. cit., 91–92.

48   Radio San Gabriel was founded in 1955 and was directed towards evangelism and literacy through programs that taught the Aymaras to read and write bilingually. It is part of the Red Erbol.

mamatallas[49]) who came from the communities. Before addressing this issue we must consider the differences between information and communication.

Maturana and Varela argue that in communication there is no "information transmitted" but only a linkage of behaviors. They question the so-called "metaphor of the tube," according to which "communication is something that is generated in one spot, carried by a conduit (or tube), and delivered to another at the receiving end." Based on field experiences and research with birds and mammals, they conclude that the communication is "coordinated behavior in a domain of structural linkage."[50] In the case of the October 2003 insurrection and other times of intense social activity, there is no unidirectional communication, but something different—the propagation of a stream (collective actions, the circulation of voices and feelings, etc.) through a set of links, each of which activates the next. Scientists call this process "circular causation" or "feedback."[51]

I postulate that a kind of communication without central emission—and therefore without passive recipients—has been critical to moving the whole of Aymara society, and keeping it mobilized until the fall of Sánchez de Lozada.[52] In effect, during those weeks the message was of crucial importance—as much what was said on air on the radio, as what was happening to those receiving the information. The hunger strike at Radio San Gabriel by a group of social leaders, including Felipe Quispe, functioned more as a node of inter-communication than as a command center giving orders to the base. Moreover, the rural and urban Aymara communities took over radio stations and transmitted their own messages, but above all, they communicated—in the deeper meaning of the term—moods, experiences, and emotions that were shared by those listening to the radio. This produced a very emotional effect similar to those who were airing it live. Thus there was a link that blurred the separation between emissaries and receivers.

A process of communication flowed during the October insurrection through the linkage (assembly, mutual understanding) of behavior among people who do not know one another but who shared

---

49   Translator's note: traditional male and female community authorities.

50   Alberto Maturana and Francisco Varela, *El árbol del conocimiento* (Madrid: Debate, 1996), 169.

51   Fritjof Carpa, *La trama de la vida* (Barcelona: Anagrama, 1998), 75–82.

52   Translator's note: Gonzalo Sánchez de Lozada was twice elected president of Bolivia, both times on the MNR ticket. During his first term (1993–1997), he initiated a series of landmark social, economic, and constitutional reforms. Elected to a second term in 2002, he resigned in October 2003 after protests related to the gas conflict. In March 2006, he resigned the leadership of the MNR.

values, codes, and ways of life. Communication is much more than what happens in and around the institutionalized media outlets — which are literally taken over by the inhabitants. What happened in hundreds of assemblies, in communities, and now also in plazas, churches, markets, neighborhood councils, and mass meetings, can be understood as collective self-education in which the people share ways of seeing the world and ways of responding to problems, expanding modes of action to be shared out among an extensive network of relationships. Here is one example among many:

> To convene the meetings they would hoist the Wiphala flag and when it was a matter of emergency, people would be summoned by firecrackers and whistles. In less than half an hour, most people would be present in order to be on the list. In times of tragedy like when there was a death, coffins were veiled in the square before being transferred to the church, with contributions of food, coca, cigarettes, and drinks during the wake. There were tears and widespread sadness, but at the same time they had more courage to fight without having to fear death.[53]

Communication between districts, between rural communities and the city, between the various local councils, and the entire population did not follow an institutional pattern or hierarchy. Communication, which is actually intercommunication or the internal communication of the Aymara nation, is where one can appreciate the multiplicity of mechanisms, canals, and channels, both formal and informal, already existing or created for the occasion. In all of them, communication appears more prominently as a form of community social relations, a body thick with multidirectional and simultaneous links, without center or a unified command.

From a communication perspective, the panorama presented in October 2003 is highly complex: there is a double dynamic that is difficult to separate. On the one hand, there is the concentration/dispersion dynamic to which we have referred before; and on the other hand there is a set of spaces that function as communication nodes (mostly plazas and churches), where the multitudes gather, later dispersing individually or collectively, creating other spaces to resist the state.

The process of concentration/dispersion is territorialized in much of the city, in an immanent and interior manner, creating nodes and links that bind but do not unite. Parallel to this, the nodes are dissolved in a multitude of initiatives agreed to at the time of the meeting, during the assembly. The plaza is the place of collective decision making and the church is that of ritual acts, but after decisions have been made and "starting with the inter-relation of information" they are dispersed by establishing neighborhood committees that organize the pickets and barricades without a fixed general criteria because "in certain moments they had to make decisions on a collective basis" without the possibility or the need to consult all mobilized.[54] The concentration/dispersion mechanism, now territorialized, reproduces itself almost infinitely, encompassing the entire urban arena.

The mechanisms of this double pulse—the succession of beats of the multitude—generate an incredible and diverse collective social energy:

> Powerful networks of action and systems of communication were activated. The different radio stations transmitting direct coverage on the events were instrumental in increasing the numbers quickly. The system of Popular Radio Television [RTP in its Spanish acronym] and Red Erbol, as well as Channels 21 and 36 on the television played a fundamental role. Many of these media outlets were threatened by the government for doing this. And they integrated themselves with the inter-neighborhood means of communication such as blowing horns and whistles or the banging of lamp-posts to communicate an imminent danger or the presence of military forces. These measures had also been used to draw attention to the presence of criminals.
>
> This is how what we define as neighborhood micro-governments emerge. Through the neighborhood organizational structures, each area of the town becomes a center for production of collective decisions in order to weave a sense of power, immobilizing the city and government.[55]

It can be added that a good number of the mechanisms of intercommunication discussed (whistles, banging) are used daily by residents to alert the community to the threat of thieves or rapists. Secondly, there is a clear lack of separation between emissaries and receptors, as well as between means of communication and community. Finally, there is no planned-out process—in the traditional sense—but a spontaneity, in the deep voluntary sense, based on les-

---

54   Ibid., 46.
55   Ibid., 41.

sons learned previously. In this way, it seems both intentional and deliberate, though lacking a pre-prepared plan imposed from outside of the movement. The plan of action, to give it some kind of name, was born within the movement and in the throes of insurrection. Sometimes, as in October 2003 in El Alto, it seems that there was a general intellect at work or, in other words, a collective common sense constructed in the heat of the action.

CHAPTER 4

State Powers and Non-state Powers: Difficult Coexistence

So far, we have described the non-state powers that we see in the social movements. It does not seem necessary to stress that these powers are mobile, not static, that they are discontinuous, not stable; and that they appear and disappear in complex situations characterized by the simultaneous withdrawal from the state and the outpouring of social relationships that form the core of the new society in movement. These factors do not bear a cause-and-effect relationship to one another (it is not the movement that—at least directly—weakens the state), but are two machines that function differently, with unique logics, and feed on relationships that have little to do with each other. Later we will see how those powers are manifest in the case of community justice—an example that could be extended to other settings, revealing that this system of justice is sustained in community relations and not by formal institutions. We have seen how non-state powers take shape during widespread mobilizations that restrain the state—and sometimes the state goes into crisis—allowing submerged relationships to become visible. But the state exists, and there is a constant attempt—especially from within the social movements—to crystallize and consolidate it as much as to impede it.

In effect, there is an ongoing social battle that is simultaneously closed and open, covering every pore of the social body; it is a struggle to impose the space-time of the state, which is that of capitalism. The system aims to disrupt the community's control—a self-control that is grounded in direct, face-to-face social relationships—to "liberate" the community from that control and to convert its members into citizens with rights and duties under the state. That is, they are carried out outside of the community space. What we see is a two-way struggle: one to assert community and difference (as a community) and the other to assert capitalism and homogeneity (equality "within" the state and the market). In this struggle, the state plays a central role in two ways: firstly, by seeking to disarm, disorganize, and disperse community social relations—this can sometimes take the form of repression, but more often it is done by making individuals submit voluntarily (the dull coercion of economic forces that Marx speaks of).

And secondly, the state disrupts the communiy's control by imposing itself upon society and especially upon social movements, provoking the emergence of a separate body that will "lead by commanding." If for the first, it acts state-like, legislating or suppressing, the second is done in a more subtle way, trying to build upon statist elements that already exist in the "other" society. That is, by disarming the ability to neutralize leaders, by spreading the latent state or the state as a possibility, it thereby weakens the mechanisms of control. In chapter two we saw that one of these mechanisms is to create basic territorial units that are considerably larger than the urbanizations with their local councils (with an average of a thousand people or 200 to 300 families),[1] encompassing neighborhoods with between five and ten thousand people (one to two thousand families). Size does matter in this case, because the state is attempting to weaken the kind of control that can only be exercised directly, face to face.

When speaking of the relationship between low population density and societies without a state, Clastres informs us that when a community reaches a certain size, part of the group separates to create another community.[2] This is a natural community self-regulation that enables the continuity of the space without the state: to increase numbers beyond a certain limit is one way to dilute community control. The experience of the social movement in the city of El Alto should be observed carefully, because it suggests that large numbers of humans can live without a state: something that has not been apparent until now and which has been a stumbling block from the standpoint of social emancipation. In other words, one way to disperse the state is to create spaces without large numbers of people, in which relations occur through face-to-face interactions. Perhaps the decreasing number of members in each neighborhood assembly (in fifteen years the number fell by thirty percent) is related to this logic, but it is too early to evaluate this fully.

We must recall that there are no societies or social spaces without the state: when we speak of non-state powers we are referring to their capacity to disperse or prevent the state from crystallizing. But that presupposes that the state is always present, otherwise it could not be established from scratch. Clastres is very clear about this:

> Yes, the state exists in primitive societies, even in the smallest group of nomadic hunters. It exists, but it is unceasingly averted, its realization constantly prevented. A primitive society is a society that directs all of its ef-

---

1   This is a project of USAID.

2   Pierre Clastres, *Society Against the State* (Caracas: Monte Avila, 1978), 186.

forts to preventing its leader from becoming *the* leader
(this can even lead to murder). If history is the history
of class struggle (in societies where there are classes, ob-
viously), then you can say that the history of societies
without classes is the history of their struggle against the
latent state, the history of their effort to codify the flows
of power.[3]

Certainly, the state exists in all social spaces, in all relations,
as power or at least as a possibility, and, furthermore, "it has always
existed."[4] Even in the rural Aymara communities, and especially in
the El Alto barrios where the exterior—the surrounding city—of the
communities is much more present. Furthermore, there is no evolu-
tion of the non-state toward the state, because it arises "whole and
in one piece;"[5] so we must identify those relationships in the heart
of the barrios that encourage state power. This is a reverse view of
that offered by Marxism: it is not the existence of classes that allows
primitive society to develop toward the state but rather the existence
of the state that allows the emergence of classes, because that is the
mechanism through which the expropriation of wealth takes place.
This is what Clastres means when he says that the state, firmly anchored in primitive society, "comes from the external, necessarily."[6]

How is the state formed in the El Alto social movement? What
are the conditions that encourage the creation of state power in El
Alto? How did this separation take shape? We believe that there are
at least two dynamics at play: one, we say, is in the interior of each
neighborhood council, and a second pertains to the movement as a
whole. The state exists, effectively, in every neighborhood council, in
every practice organized in a structured way, but the residents have
also developed mechanisms to address this. In many cases they fail,
even temporarily; sometimes they achieve partial successes—not as
a result of an explicit struggle with this goal in mind, but through
more subtle and therefore more effective mechanisms: camouflaged
desertion, apathy, disinterest, and reluctance, practices in which the
Indians have been training themselves for some 500 years—to the
despair of colonizers. On other occasions, especially after the year
2000, the rebellious outpouring appears to have been the dominant
way to neutralize statist pressures within the social movements. In

---

3   In Gilles Deleuze, *La isla desierta* (Valencia: Pre-Textos, 2005), 292.

4   Asserted by Gilles Deleuze and Félix Guattari in *El Anti Edipo* (Buenos
Aires: Paidós, 1985).

5   Gilles Deleuze, *La isla desierta*, ibid., 292.

6   Ibid.

any case, it is necessary to look in more detail at how the state grows within the movement.

Neighborhood Councils as Institutions

The institutionalization of social movements is one way of establishing state powers, in which the leaders—or the bodies of leaders—are separated from the movement as a whole. The establishment of these leadership bodies consolidates the separation between leaders and led, creating leaders who no longer "lead by obeying" but "lead by commanding." So, the institutionalization of social movements is a vital step toward producing separation. This is how the process looks from above. From below, the need to institutionalize movements arises when impotency appears or the power to act weakens, which is closely linked to demobilization or ebbs in militancy in which residents leave the management of local councils to the supervisory commission. To be sure, the local community can control, and indeed does control, the leadership through the framework of the monthly or weekly assemblies, but often these same meetings are overly formal and the ability to control them escapes the neighbors. This can be said another way: the disengaged movement (disengaged from the functional place in the system) arrives at its own limits and thus becomes a movement institution.

The neighborhood councils are not identical with the barrio community, but are rather the way that it represents to others, particularly the state. This is a first separation that we must bear in mind: it explains why the councils had to be transcended in October 2003 to lead to an insurrection. The neighborhood councils are subject to a type of separation that is a requirement of the Law of Popular Participation [LPP, in its Spanish acronym], which imposes certain standards of internal organization without which they will not receive legal status. The municipal government recognizes the urbanizations that meet certain legal requirements and, finally, the FEJUVE also imposes certain conditions: it demands a legally adopted municipal resolution and, this is very important, a minimum of 200 families or 400 lots.[7] The LPP compelled changes in internal organization and in the statutes, even obliging the councils to have women in the leadership.[8] The Organic Statute of the FEJUVE recognized that the neighborhood organization operates under the pro-

---

7   Article 72, points a) and b) of the Organic Statute of FEJUVE El Alto of 2003.

8   The Supreme Decree N° 24.447, December 20th 1996, provides in Article 5: "Gender Equity—In shaping its directives, the Base Territorial Organizations should promote the participation of citizens of both sexes."

visions of the Popular Participation Law, the Supreme Regulatory Decree 23858, and the Municipalities Law.[9]

As a result of the state regulation, all of the grassroots territorial organizations are strongly institutionalized. The FEJUVE, for example, has an executive committee, which is the leadership organ with twenty-nine ministries, including president and vice president, elected every two years by a congress that must be recognized by the CONALJUVE (national organization of neighborhood councils). The neighborhood councils tend to have an average of sixteen secretariats; each council has one representative in the districts in which the city is divided up, and the districts have participation in the Executive according to proportional quotas. The monthly or weekly assemblies are or should be occasions for the participation and decision of all the neighbors. All work and duties are regulated by the Organic Statute.

In addition, the legislation provides for the creation of the Supervisory Committee that decides on the Municipal Development Plan, the Annual Operating Plan, and the physical execution and budgeting for them both.[10] The supervisory committees are important components in the relationships between local councils and the state, particularly with the municipality, which is responsible for providing many of the services which, in turn, hold together the barrio. The law defines the supervisory committee as "an institution of civil society" and even acknowledges that "its structure and functioning are independent of public bodies, who should refrain from interfering in its management." Even more, they concede it the power to "control and supervise Municipal Government resources."[11]

A central element in the institutionalization of any movement is the establishment of formal representatives. In this case, besides the regulation of neighborhood councils, legislation provides that the relationships between them and the state are mediated through representatives. One aspect that indicates the separation between the structure of the local councils and the barrio appears in the statutes of FEJUVE: for each congress of the organization, local councils may accredit four delegates, "two delegates from the leadership and two from the base, elected by the assembly."[12] The bases have the same representation as the leadership of the council. Although the assembly elects those who serve on the council, they are typically people with certain characteristics:

---

9   FEJUVE, Organic Statute of 2003, 15.

10 Supreme Decree N° 24.447, article 14.

11 Ibid., articles 15 and 16.

12 Organic Statute of the FEJUVE of 2003, art. 16, subsection c), 23.

A council has a president, a secretary of minutes, sports, and finance, because they do the paperwork to get water, light, drainage, sidewalks, gas installations, schools, sports fields.... They meet monthly and these councils are like those in the rural communities. *The leaders are those who speak eloquently or have some experience in networking.* Initially, these positions went to people coming from La Paz.[13]

This indicates that not everyone can be elected as leader of the neighborhood council. In principle, rotation and *obligatoriness* does not function in this setting the same as it does in the community. In the 1980s there was a "relative isolation of the neighborhood councils with respect to their bases" largely because the leaders had economic advantages, social prestige, and political power.[14] There had been a lot of emphasis on the existence of *clientelism* in the relationship between neighborhood leaders and political parties and the state, resulting in the co-optation of the neighborhood leaders.

The requirements imposed by local councils and FEJUVE for the election of leaders (i.e., not to be a real estate speculator; not to have links with the law or be a baker, trader, transporter, or political party leader; not to have abandoned one's duties as a leader; not to be a traitor, or have participated in dictatorships) appear to limit or control the leaders.[15] However, this set of conditions did not work, because in the decade after its adoption, the 1990s, the FEJUVE was entirely subordinate to the municipal government of CONDEPA (Conciencia de Patria / Conscience of the Nation) and several of its leaders were members of political parties and even municipal officials, which violated the rules of the organization.

In any case, in the late 1980s, a clear separation predominated between the leaders of the local councils and the neighborhood grassroots. Some residents noted the existence of "an elitist vision of the councils," and "an ambivalent relationship between bases and leaders, where the former occasionally identified with their organization and the latter occasionally shared decisions."[16] In the mid-1980s, the separation between FEJUVE and the base was clear as it had put aside local residents' demand to become an area of struggle between the political parties seeking control of the organization. A FEJUVE communiqué from March 1985 reveals that division: "The

---

13. Interview with Pablo Mamani Ramirez. My emphasis.

14. Sandóval and Sostres, *La ciudad prometida*, ibid., 81.

15. Ibid., 82. In the statutes adopted in 2003 the reference to treason and collaboration with dictatorships have disappeared.

16. Ibid., 83.

neighborhood leaders urged the political parties 'to refrain' from dividing the residents of El Alto with its practice of fighting an 'open battle' for people's votes, offering groceries, peoples' pharmacies, free clinics."[17]

Despite the criticism, FEJUVE did not question the practice, but only the "opportunism" it represented by doing this during the pre-election period, which is when they issued the statement. According to FEJUVE, "what is right and moral" would be that the parties oversaw works even beyond the election period. Note that they attribute the practice of dividing or buying of volunteers to forces outside the neighborhood, as if the leaders were passive objects engaged in struggles beyond their control. In fact, from the very moment that many of them were appointed, many aspired to and participated in the colonial policy of exchanging favors for votes.

In the late 1980s, there was a growing tendency toward autonomy within the El Alto neighborhood movement, partly because of the democratizing impulse experienced within the country from 1982 onwards, as well as due to the relocation of thousands of miners to the city in 1985 and thereafter. It seems that the First Extraordinary Congress of FEJUVE in 1983 prompted "a new style of teamwork" that tended toward "decentralization of the decision making level."[18] Some analyses emphasize the influence of the union culture in the neighborhood movement, which would have given it a centralized character, which the statutes define as "democratic centralism." However, it is possible that this may also come from the hegemonic statist culture in the Bolivian popular movement.

The migration of some six thousand mining families to El Alto must have had a role in changing this state of affairs. That sector bore social characteristics that differentiate it from the inhabitants of El Alto: the educational level of the relocated miners is above the nation's average, as much among men as women and children. To this, we must add the experience of struggle and organization in the mining unions, given that more than half of those who settled in El Alto had worked at least fifteen years in the mines.[19] These characteristics coalesce in a somewhat different socio-political culture and, especially, a knowledge of organizational capacity far more autonomous from the state and political parties. It was apparently these miners who played a decisive role in the mobilization of local councils and the FEJUVE. The miners were well aware of their ability to orga-

---

17   FEJUVE Communique El Alto, March 4 1985, in Sandóval and Sostres, *La ciudad prometida*, 93.

18   Sandóval and Sostres, *La ciudad prometida*, 97.

19   Ibid, 175–177.

nize and expressed it on various occasions.[20] The residents, at least those in some neighborhoods, showed deference to and admiration for the miners' "deeds" and learned from their experiences.[21]

In any case, Sandoval and Sostres's analysis seems apt in the sense that the democratization of FEJUVE put a brake on the double role of "being on the one hand, a barrio spokesperson, and on the other, a partner in the state's operations in this city, and in this way playing the role of intermediary between the neighborhood councils and the state."[22] In effect, part of the work of the local councils is to "participate in the preparation of district plans and programs (Municipal Development Plan, District Development Plan, Annual Operating Plan)," and "to cooperate with central, departmental, and local government and other institutions to improve the Sustainable Human Development of its inhabitants," among the most emphasized.[23] Such tasks are assigned to the neighborhood councils and the FEJUVE, thought necessary for the improvement of the neighborhoods, but—on the contrary—serving to intensify the separation of a body of representatives that are only as much in contact with their bases as with state institutions and political parties, with whom they establish fluid relationships. Over the years these relationships with the state and political parties tend to become even stronger and more stable than those maintained with the grassroots, generating habits and lifestyles that differ from the rest of the local inhabitants, who have no access to such spaces.

In El Alto, the act of being leader has become something almost suspect. Indeed, complaints about cases of corruption or political maneuvering (especially among electoral candidates) are quite common, though not always properly substantiated. According to testimonies, some of those allegations could be part of a fight for power within FEJUVE or for places on electoral ballots. In any case, the act of denouncing leadership—amplified by the popular media—shows that the grassroots have the ability to control their leaders, as we shall see below.

• • • • • • • • • • • • •

---

20   See testimony of miners relocated in Sandóval and Sostres, *La ciudad prometida*, 162 and 163.

21   "The neighbors have learned a lot from the ex-miners because they had every opportunity to share their exploits. This fighting spirit helped years later to start the demonstrations in the University." Marco Quispe, *De ch'usa marka a jach'a marka*, 99.

22   Ibid., 97–98.

23   Art. 71, paragraph a) and art. 6 paragraph f) of the FEJUVE Organic Statute of 2003.

The 1990s experienced a major political shift with the triumph of the CONDEPA in winning the El Alto mayor's office, which advocated municipal autonomy for the first time in the 1987 elections. It is worth dwelling on this decade of CONDEPA dominance because its collapse coincides with the cycle of struggles launched from 2000 onwards. CONDEPA was the embodiment of Aymara political, social, and cultural ascendance.[24] The massive vote for CONDEPA in the 1989 national and municipal elections (in El Alto they won 65 percent of the votes, a percentage that remained steady throughout the decade), pushing aside traditional political parties and leaving them with ten percent of the vote, which should be read as a community decision—because of the size and force of the swing—indicating that social relations exist in El Alto that still, as pointed out by several authors, operate according to the logic of Andean reciprocity and distribution.[25] "The establishment of a strong cultural identity among El Alto residents has been expressed in collective voting patterns," says Quisbert, manifesting itself in a kind of "ideological loyalty" to those who value the Andean culture.[26]

The CONDEPA formed as a result of the ruling class offensive led by the Nationalist Revolutionary Movement (MNR—Movimiento Nacionalista Revolucionario) government, which shut down the communications media of the popular broadcaster and singer Carlos Palenque in 1988. The popular sectors of El Alto and La Paz, basically the Aymaras, mobilized to press for the reopening of Radio Metropolitana and Channel 4, which made up the Popular Radio Television (RTP in its Spanish acronym). For over two decades, Palenque wove a vast network of loyalties based on personal and family relationships that were activated with the formation of the CONDEPA, an organization that "embodied the social sectors neglected and ignored by the Creole elite that monopolizes official culture, and denounced the injustices of the prevailing order in the name of those excluded from the economic, social, political, and cultural life of the country."[27]

CONDEPA had a social base made up of migrants, impoverished teachers, housewives, artisans, traders, domestic workers,

---

24   On the subject there is a fairly extensive bibliography. We highlight the work of Marcos Quisbert Quispe (2003), Rafael Archondo (1991) and Joaqua Saravia and Godofredo Sandóval (1991).

25   See the work of Rafael Archondo (already cited) and Joaqua Saravia and Godofredo Sandóval, *Jach'a Uru: la esperanza de un pueblo. Carlos Palenque RTP y los sectores populares urbanos en La Paz* (La Paz: CEP-ILDIS, 1991).

26   Marco Quisbert, *FEJUVE El Alto 1990–1998* (La Paz: Aruwiyiri, 2003), 66.

27   Ibid., 53.

unemployed, and workers, and promoted reciprocity and Andean culture. According to Archondo, the People's Radio and Television System (RTP) was based on three characteristics: solidarity, equality for migrants, and a strong criticism of the political class, particularly the MNR, given that expressing the culture of the oppressed required a confrontation with the colonial political system.

Although CONDEPA has been analyzed from the perspective of clientelism and de-ideologization—as in prioritizing intimate personal ties and converting them into political solidarity as a means of solving practical problems—other core aspects should be considered as well. It arose as part of a process of discrediting the traditional political parties and hastened their demise. Suddenly those from below appeared on the political spectrum as themselves without masks, like the "*pollera* women"[28] (such as "Comadre Remedios" who headed parliamentary lists) and the Aymara symbols: in a word, the Andean cosmovision had made a political entrance. Regarding the role of Carlos Palenque, no one has summarized it more beautifully than Rafael Archondo:

> To successfully convene them, he touched the most remote keys of his community soul, established the norms of solidarity, recreated dialogue and discussion among the homeless, and shared consolation and hope from the microphone; he embodied the new Andean siege, like Tupac Katari, but this one with walls of adobe and brick, calamine roofs, awnings, and even blue nylon TV antennas. In this way, the miracle that took effect liquidated the collective anguish, by giving way to the metropolitan resurrection of the *ayllu*. The community, disconcerted by urban rootlessness, began breathing again, but this time within the centralized, authoritarian, and vertical limits of the metropolis.[29]

In any case, the mobilization that led to the creation of CONDEPA as a popular reaction to the closure of RTP was a plebeian action, born and carried out from below, not dictated from above—at least not until the 1989 election campaign, when the intellectuals and professionals showed up. This movement embodies the rise of the urban Aymara and their slow conversion into subjects. An example is the case of the women: Remedios Loza was twenty-four years old, and the first "*pollera* woman" to host a show on television, in 1974; she began working on a radio program at the age of twenty, a

---

28   Translator's note: *Pollera* refers to a traditional dress worn by Aymara women.

29   Rafael Archondo, *Compadres al micrófono*, ibid.

feat few Aymaras believed could even have believed possible.[30] This is a generation of young Aymara women, born in the city, educated, but who have not abandoned their indigenous identities. In passing, we note that *comadre* Remedios, who would later become the first *pollera* deputy in the history of Bolivia, made her television appearance just a few months after a group of (male) Aymara intellectuals issued the *Manifesto of Tiwanaku* (1973). She also took the radio microphone in hand for the first time the same year as the publication of Fausto Reinaga's *The Indian Revolution* and *The Manifesto of the Indian Party of Bolivia* (1970). A decade later, as part of the movement for the reopening of RTP, dozens of Aymara women — such as Marcela Machaca — became active as leaders.[31]

But there is something even more remarkable. In the midst of a crisis of the left, popular organizations, and unions, the Aymara mobilization modified the dominant forms of social protest of that time. These changes had already been refined when Carlos Palenque was jailed for the first time in 1979. The market women took the initiative and broke him out of police custody — in the midst of a full-on dictatorship![32] Where there is mass action, when they carve neighborhood leaders from the base in El Alto and on the slopes of La Paz, a shift has occurred that anticipates the forms of social action that will later take place in the insurrection in 2003. A huge march to the Plaza de San Francisco was convened when the RTP was closed down in June 1988. "Defense committee," composed of so-called "informal" workers and grassroots neighborhood leaders, led the mobilization:

> The usual route of the march, generally organized by the COB or the political parties, has been changed by the defense committee. Instead of traversing, as has been the tradition, the central artery of the city, the multitude leaves from the central station, reaches Buenos Aires Avenue, turns off by Tumusla and then goes down to the Juares Eguino plaza until it reaches the heart of city: Plaza San Francisco. . . . In that way, an initially small mobilization snowballed as it passed through the market stalls and the busiest streets used by the urban Aymaras, ending in a full occupation of the La Paz city center. The march went through key retail areas, led by

---

30   "It is said that at the time some of the audience were skeptical that a traditionally dressed woman such as Remedios Loza was using a radio microphone." Rafael Archondo, *Compadres al micrófono*, ibid., 153.

31   Ibid., 186.

32   Ibid., 157.

the dark conqueror from Chuquiagu, Carlos Palenque, *and descended like an unstoppable torrent* in full view of the authorities.[33]

During the powerful moments when vast popular sectors get involved in social struggle, the following phenomenon seems to occur: they change the forms of action prevailing up to then. The pattern of action instituted by the mining workers around the time of the 1952 revolution—large demonstrations in the main avenue (the Prado)—was changed when new players, the urban Aymara, emerged in 1988. Fifteen years later, in October 2003, the mobilization that toppled Gonzalo Sánchez de Lozada had very similar characteristics, despite some differences.[34]

The change at the macro level came at the same time as equally profound changes occurred at a local level. With the second closure of RTP on November 7, 1988, a group of agents from the Interior Ministry deactivated the Metropolitan radio antenna in Pampahasi. The reaction of the people was immediate: "the residents, armed with sticks and stones, forced the officers to flee hurriedly toward the town of Chicani," and the officers very narrowly escaped a lynching. Then people "decided to block the access routes to the area to prevent another similar attack." People stood guard, slept in the open and "ate in turn-around soup kitchens organized by housewives."[35]

The old pattern of social action began with a strike in a workplace, backed by a general strike and demonstrations. In the new pattern of action, the mobilization starts in the spaces of everyday life and survival (markets, neighborhoods) putting in movement an increasing number of social networks or, that is to say, societies in movement, self-articulated from within. And not laying siege, as transpired under colonialism two centuries ago, but rather boring from within until cracks emerge and, later, partially smashing the system.

This lengthy detour is an attempt to offer a long-term perspective on what lies behind and below the birth of CONDEPA and its overwhelming victory in El Alto. The co-optation of the FEJUVE leaders and the COR by CONDEPA and the mayor's office in their hands, was very different from the co-optation of similar structures by the MNR in the wake of the 1952 revolution. There is something

---

33   Ibid., 187. My emphasis.

34   The description of the large demonstration of October 2003 states: "The west side of La Paz seemed like an anthill for an hour: every street, avenue, and road was filled by thousands who came down from the hills. The deployment was total and the contingents were crossing the steep routes in tight masses." Luis Gómez, *El Alto de pie*, 141.

35   Rafael Archondo, *Compadres to the microphone*, ibid., 208.

in common here—they occur at a time when new social subjects are growing and it becomes a way of disciplining them—but the difference, which is not minor, is that the co-optation of CONDEPA was overseen in and under the codes of the Andean cosmovision and not within those of the Western culture, as had happened after 1952. Furthermore, and this is something quite fundamental, this occurred in a period of state decline, when the colonial elites were not only retreating but the state that they had constructed was suffering a delegitimization and losing its ability to discipline and subordinate.

In this new scenario, which is frankly unfavorable for the elites and favorable for the oppressed, the 1990s were a sort of parenthesis for the insurgency begun by the urban Aymara, and also an intense period of internal development, which changes in the forms of protest reveal. It is during this period that villas or townships reduced the number of their members by a third, thus strengthening their communities, as we have seen before. Continuing along this line, we must uncover what was happening in this decade that concludes with major insurgencies.

On the one hand, CONDEPA became a party of order. It established alliances with former dictator Hugo Banzer and the ADN (Nationalist Democratic Alliance) and was accepted as a political force within the system. From the mayor's office in El Alto, it used patronage networks and friendships to establish vertical loyalties, based on cultural identification between the Aymara people and their leaders. The emergence of CONDEPA and the simultaneous realization of genuine elections all over the country brought about a real redistribution and expansion of power, resulting in the fact that previously displaced sectors assumed local power.[36] From the point of view of the social movement, the new statist configuration in El Alto caused the subordination and co-optation of the leaders. "The political parties, acting as mediation structures, established practices that introduced the possibility of clientelist connections, impacting the local organizations, which represented a new space of influence and manipulation," points out Quisbert.[37]

The overall picture of the decade is twofold: co-optation of the movements into institutions (or their leaders through perks and the grassroots through concessions received as clients) and, parallel to this, neighborhood action to control their own organizations and leaders. In the background, control by means of co-optation is fleeting and incomplete, because it does not reach all of the organizations throughout the city—there are not enough resources to accommodate so many unmet needs. The unions lost their capacity to exert

---

36 Marco Quisbert, *FEJUVE El Alto 1990–1998*, 69.
37 Ibid.

autonomous pressure and the FEJUVE lost "the ability to keep operating as an organic civic structure. "[38]

Competition between political parties to subordinate the movement resulted in its division: in 1994, the Federation of Retail Traders had two leaderships: one identified with CONDEPA and the other with UCS (Unidad Civica Solidaridad—Civic Unity Solidarity). In 1992, FEJUVE divided under pressure from the UCS and the Patriotic Agreement (ADN-MIR). In 1998, FEJUVE underwent another division, this time forming two federations, due to competition between CONDEPA and other parties who were trying to displace it—a division that remained until mid-June, 1999.[39] But this is just what happened in the institutions, problems that intensify during election periods. In reality, the whole decade reveals a panorama of intense struggle: for the leadership of the local councils and the unions to have control of the grassroots communities and for the communities to maintain their own control.

We note some counter-tendencies. One of them, the most basic, has a "legal" character and tries to insert into the organizations' statutes requirements that leaders cannot be municipal officials or electoral candidates for political parties. In general, these measures don't work, and are circumvented in the same way that community control is circumvented. At other times, the movement made specific calls for candidates to renounce their leadership positions. This happened in almost all election campaigns and, beyond the results achieved, shows that there is some kind of control exercised by the bases—although unclear and inefficient on many occasions. Sometimes the forms of control are very oblique, especially when grassroots movements are undergoing moments of great weakness. In 1992, when FEJUVE divided, the bases in several neighborhoods also divided—not as a reflection of what was happening "above," but as a strategy. Thus, in Villa Pacajes, "as the leaders of this area, we have also divided, in order to distribute ourselves in both conferences, so that we could play an important role through FEJUVE and not support any of the conflicting tendencies."[40]

There is another example of the base remedying this situation collectively. In 1992, the El Alto Assembly was created. Born in an informal way (people don't even remember when or how), it had no legal standing, but neighborhood organizations and labor unions found a voice within the assembly and it took on a diversity of issues within the city. After overseeing important actions such as the strike on March 6, 1997—supported by officials in the mayor's office and

---

38   Ibid.
39   Ibid., 81–100.
40   Ibid., 84.

all social sectors—that demanded more resources for the city, the construction of a hospital, and an airport transfer service; these being the most prominent demands among others. They articulated the diversity of the various actors, and "occasionally tried to overcome the fragmentation of social demands caused by the clientelism rife in City Hall" and became a force that combated both co-optation and CONDEPA's persecution of those community leaders who would not submit. In sum, the El Alto Assembly was a resource for the neighborhood and union leaders who acted on behalf of the people to fight the overpowering advance of CONDEPA during these years— although some activists here were merely competing for the patronage of CONDEPA. The Assembly stopped functioning during the conflicts in 2003. Or to put it another way, the rise of social struggles meant that mechanisms such as the El Alto Assembly were no longer required, and it was transcended.[41]

Finally, the general impression is one of generational turnover coupled with growing dissatisfaction with the patronage system (and a widening of the social movement demands to include water and gas), pushing aside and breaking the mechanisms of co-optation. In this process, the consolidation of the barrio communities and their growing politicization—to the point of taking the initiative on the debates about water management and nationalization of hydrocarbons—appears to have merged into the FEJUVE Congress of 1999, representing an important turning point.

On the one hand, CONDEPA disappeared. Carlos Palenque died in 1997 and by the 2002 elections his social base has vanished. As a result, the loyalties of his "clients" fell apart, having no vertical reference point left, as the CONDEPA could not hold the networks together in the absence of their senior leader. In addition, a cleft appeared in the hills that would have immediate relevance.

But maybe what really matters in this case is what is happening at the grassroots. According to several interviewees, El Alto would have erupted in the early '90s, when the conditions for this were ripe, but for the efforts of CONDEPA to prevent this. It seemed that "the city was immobilized for ten years, tightly controlled and gagged, the suppression reaching even as far as Pepelucho (Mayor José Luis Paredes, of the MIR). Eventually it could no longer be contained and it had to erupt. El Alto began to explode around 2003 with the Maya and Paya taxes."[42] In Julio Mamani Conde's view, the phenomenal growth of the city since 1990 increased the pressure from below, and in parallel, "the experience of CONDEPA served as a lesson. Congress ensured that leaders should have no relation to

---

41   Ibid., 72–73.

42   Interview with Julio Mamani Conde.

the Mayor's office when exercising their duties; that is, to make it so that it won't happen again."

But the most important aspect of the turnaround in 2000 was the emergence of a new generation of youth. There is a general understanding that the "UPEA (Public University of El Alto) generation" that appeared on the scene in the late 90s and was formed by the pressure and social mobilization in 2003:

> *Without the UPEA movement, all the movements would have been divided.* People have been calling for a university since our parents' time. They believed that their children should not be denied education like them. From 1989 onwards, the clamor for a University of El Alto increased, and we began to gather the building materials. The first point of negotiation we demanded was for the UMSA [43] of La Paz to oversee the process, but they believed that El Alto was second class and in the end only threw us two technical courses, one in mechanics. And that was a disappointment, because people wanted more than mechanics—it is not enough. The UMSA made no effort to create the University of El Alto.
>
> Palenque died in 1997, around the same time that these young people emerged, who were willing to take up the struggle for the university. It was a pressure from below. They formed the organizations. The leaders of these organizations were highly suspect, because the political parties had been interfering in them since 1998, pretty scandalous things like parliamentary deputies circulating around the movement congresses. The biggest FEJUVE congress was held in 1999. I went to four conferences, and the 1999 one was historic, with around 1,200 people convoked. Before this congress, attendance numbers were nominal, and the only time they were there was when it was time to appoint the leadership. Documents were not discussed here, and the first commissions functioned here. This congress was a turning point; there was strong pressure exerted from below. The ten years of CONDEPA was the lost decade during which no work was done. CONDEPA helped enhance the self-esteem of the Indians, because from that moment on the Indian was no longer ashamed as before, but at the same time there was gradual pressure from the social base to

---

43   Translator's note: Universidad Mayor de San Andrés of La Paz.

improve their organizations. In 2000–2001, they started to organize the movement with Cori.[44]

This pressure "from below" is also related to generational change. Young people had been mostly confined to parish-run youth centers. But they began expanding their activities throughout the '90s, through communications media, radio, the popular reporters center, and music. Plazas became meeting spaces for the youth, and included debate and learning. "The push came from the cultural centers that began to open in the neighborhood; they were accepted by the neighborhood and are now part of it."[45] Up to 1999, the vast majority of the leaders were fifty or older, many of them retirees with time to devote to the work of local councils; but then, around this time, students and teachers began to get involved. According to Marco Quispe, rather than a generational turnover, "it is an encounter between the UPEA youth, other young people who have a more diffuse but no less effective presence, and the adults."

Heading into the new century, the stage is set for the barrio communities to overstep the neighborhood councils. It is indeed difficult to believe that the old system of clientelism has disappeared. The current majority who are with the MAS could well reproduce the old molds or create new forms of clientelist relations. In any case, the image we want to project is of a dynamic of relationships and a state of flux. No process can move from a state of total co-optation to a state of autonomy; there are changes and ruptures and continuities, always linked to the involvement of, or disconnections with, local communities. We must stress these lines of fissure—breaks such as those that occurred between 1970–1974, 1988–1989, and 2000–2003. Regarding the specific issue of co-optation, note that less than a decade passed between the initial triumph of CONDEPA and its demise in 1989–1991. If we compare what happened in this period with the post-1952 period up to the breakdown of the military/rural farmers pact in the 1970s, it must be concluded that the movement's vulnerability to co-optation and neutralization by the state has significantly declined. These findings are important in a pivotal time like right now, in which there has been a transcendent change in those individuals running the Bolivian government.

In any case, it is clear that barrio residents are learning to counter the new forms of state subordination. Since 2002, with the change of leadership and Cori assuming the presidency of FEJUVE, the *ampliados* (assemblies of leaders of the neighborhood councils) are beginning to make the important decisions in an effort to prevent

---

44   Interview with Marco Quispe. My emphasis.
45   Ibid.

the organization from being monopolized by the small core of the directive, a situation that had led to numerous acts of corruption.[46] Still, this type of control is unsatisfactory and requires constant vigilance. After October 2003, a series of divisions occurred in the FE-JUVE leadership and now it is more difficult for leaders to operate behind the backs of the people. In August 2004, "Mauricio Cori was beaten and had to walk the streets of El Alto half-naked," accused of secretly negotiating for jobs in the El Alto and La Paz municipalities and with a state company.[47] This practice, borrowed from the rural communities, reveals that the urban neighborhood communities are becoming a force. It also reveals that the battle for control and autonomy fought out between the base and the leadership (which is actually a manifestation of the concentration-dispersion struggle) has no end; it is a permanent struggle because—as Clastres noted—the state always exists, although in some societies it is endlessly thwarted.

Movement as Institution and as a Moving-of-itself

The organic unity of the movement—different from the confluence of unity from below—is a statist form of social mobilization. The mobilization of the popular sectors often occurs horizontally, while that of the elite is done vertically.[48] The oppressed mobilize vertically when they are accompanying or following mobilizations of those above, such as what occurs during elections. When we talk of the mobilization of the subordinate, we are talking about a mobilization born from below and directed from below, usually without recognized and formal leaders but led by "natural" leaders recognized by those from below: that is, people just like them.

There is a large body of work dealing with social movements that focuses, as a whole, on three questions: organization, collective identity, and codes of mobilization.[49] This view is hegemonic in the sociology of social movements and, accordingly, gives priority to aspects of the movements like structure, cohesion, and definition of objectives.[50] To be considered in this way, movements must have an organization that is different from that which preceded its emergence, because social relations immersed in the daily lives of the people are not regarded as organization per se. They should have a common

---

46   Interview with Julio Mamani Conde.

47   Cited by Pablo Mamani in *Microgobiernos barriales*, 80.

48   Ranahit Guha, *Las voces de la historia*, 37.

49   Alvaro García Linera, *Sociología de los movimientos sociales en Bolivia*, 21–22.

50   See Godofredo Sandoval et al, *Chukiyawa. La cara aymara de La Paz. Nuevos lazos con el campo* (La Paz: CIPCA, 1987), 179.

goal (García Linera); minimum standards of cohesion (Sandoval et al); and finally, present strategic (García Linera) or well-defined objectives (Sandoval et al).

Movements are therefore framed as homogeneous, collective actors, with defined interests and rational forms of action appropriate to the aims pursued. If this formula has ever functioned, it was during the period when mass-trade unions and centralized syndicates dominated, but it is doubtful that the miners who participated in the 1952 revolution had been inspired by the *Tesis de Pulacayo*—which surely the vast majority had not read before the events, despite the clear value of the work.

A kind of epistemological earthquake occurs when those who have occupied the depths of society for centuries—Indians and women, etc.—emerge as subjects, which calls into question the subject/object relationship, one of the most pernicious legacies of colonialism.[51] This relationship is reflected, among many others, in what Guha Ranajit defined as "the univocity of statist discourse" that "sees a particular set of contradictions as dominant or central and the need to resolve them as a priority or more urgent then all the others."[52] It is because of this argument that those of "the low voices" (women, Indians, etc.) were not taken into account for centuries. It brings to mind the recuperation of a vision of the world very similar to that of the Indian and indigenist elite of the Movement for Socialism (MAS).

In effect, the MAS organization issued a statement that expresses strong empathy with the modernization project emanating from above after the 1952 revolution. For the principal intellectual of the MAS, Alvaro García Linera, "the social movement cannot manage or occupy the state" because the logic of the movement is to decentralize decision making while the government has to concentrate this capacity, rendering the social movement unfit for government— which is why they should cede this power to politicians, intellectuals, and party professionals. But, in addition, he argues that "the state is the only rational force in Bolivia." Therefore, he argues that "every struggle goes through the state; even the struggle against the state passes through the state."[53] In sum, according to this view, there is no way of escaping the institutionalization of any struggle, including that for emancipation, which by definition is a process on the mar-

---

51   This theme is developed here: Raúl Zibechi, *La emancipación como producción de vínculos* (Buenos Aires: Clacso, 2005).

52   Ranajit Guha, *Las voces de la historia*, 30. For "statist" is understood as "an ideology for which the State is at the center of history." ibid., 17.

53   Alvaro García Linera, interview in the periodical *Pensamiento y movimientos sociales en América Latina*, Niteroi, 15 October, 2005.

gin and against state institutions. This view of the political responds to a strategy that clearly defines enemies and principal contradictions ("first we will face the petrol bosses and when we've resolved this contradiction we will deal with the others," says García Linera), which is to know the differences and separate the secondary, in a kind of rationalization of social activity that we define as "statist." Nevertheless, the MAS's modernist outlook goes much further:

> The future of Bolivia is the modern, not the familial economy. In El Alto, sixty soldiers killed seventy people in a half an hour. Until you have modernity on your side, you cannot succeed. The pre-modern cannot succeed. The traditional and the local are fruits of domination. To eulogize the local and traditional is to eulogize domination. The World Bank promotes the local.[54]

This type of analysis is based on "a certain order of consistency and linearity ... that dictates what should be included in history and what should be left out."[55] And apparently this should be the fate of the so-called pre-modern, such as the traditional and the local — just as the indigenous movements have been disregarded in recent decades. In other words, the Andean world as we know it, the world that its inhabitants have built in their five centuries of resistance, is itself only a reminiscence from the past, fated to disappear at the altar of modernity and socialism.

This vision of the movement is not able to go beyond the systems of the state, which prevents it from hearing the "quiet voices submerged by the noisy state mandates," and even less "to interact with them."[56] If we put aside the conception of history and society implied by this analysis and focus instead on the issue of social movements, we see that they are considered incomplete and inadequate, and must be completed and led by parties that are part of the state system. In this case, the "pre-modern" ranks with the "spontaneous" in the classic Marxist analysis: the point of convergence is that the pre-modern as much as the spontaneous are the opposite of the rational (the state, the party), and in both cases the movements of the oppressed themselves are thought unable to create the new world. That can only be done from the perspective of the state and with Western rationality.

At this point, the road forks: we either accept that the oppressed have their own autonomous political capacities or label their activity "spontaneous;" that is, politically blind, not conscious

---

54   Ibid.
55   Ranahit Guha, *Las voces de la historia*, ibid., 31.
56   Ibid., 20.

or structured, as in, unconscious and pre-political. Guha, following Gramsci, says that using the word "spontaneous" is elitist because it responds to a scholastic and academic historico-political perspective that "defines as real and worthy of consideration only for rebel movements that are 100 percent conscientious, meaning the movements that are directed by plans prepared in advance to the last detail, or situated along an abstract theoretical line."[57]

The Indian historian Guha says that there was nothing spontaneous in the peasant uprisings, in the sense that they were not reckless, and that "the peasants knew what they were doing when they revolted."[58] And they had carefully prepared their actions, only that it was all outside of the usual established channels, outside of the institutional framework of the state:

> In most cases, consultations between peasants who depend on the various organizational forms of the local society where they start off, precede a revolt. There are assemblies of the clan elders and caste *panchayats* (councils), neighbors' conventions, larger mass meetings, etc. These consultation processes are often very lengthy and can last weeks or even months before reaching the necessary consensus at various levels until the majority of an entire community is mobilized by the systematic use of basic channels and media that are very different, from verbal to non-verbal communication.[59]

There is, of course, another way of addressing the social movements of the oppressed; it is not a gaze from above—taking the state as its starting point—in a colonial form. It consists of beginning with social relationships created from below for basic survival, meaning the "pre-modern" or familial relationships, and assuming as a starting point the movements of that society, their flow, their faults. Because what is a movement but this—self-movement? "Every social movement is configured by those who wish to rupture social inertia and move themselves, which is to say *they change places*, refusing the place they have been historically assigned within a given social organization, and broaden their spaces for expression."[60] Porto Gonçalves reached this conclusion after working for years with the *seringueiros* (rubber extractors) from the Amazon jungle, together with Chico Mendes, who was their adviser.

---

57   Ibid., 99.

58   Ibid., 104.

59   Ibid.

60   Carlos Walter Porto Gonçalves, *Geo-grafías* (México: Siglo XXI, 2001), 81.

We are talking about giving priority to the shift over the structure, or the mobile over the fixed, to the society flowing as opposed to the state, which seeks to codify and control the flow. In this analysis, the movement's objectives do not derive from the place they occupy in the society (worker, peasant, or Indian, etc.) nor the program advanced, nor the statements or intensity of the mobilizations. It does not judge the movement according to its organizational "solidity," its degree of centralization or homogeneity—things that would speak about the strength of its organic structure.

We do not discount these fragmented or dispersed movements but rather propose to address these characteristics from an immanent gaze. Again and again, non-articulated and non-unified movements have been capable of doing many things: toppling governments, liberating large regions from the state's presence, creating different ways of living beyond the hegemonic, and waging important daily battles for the survival of the oppressed. Social change, the creation and recreation of social bonds, does not need articulation, centralization, or unification. Moreover, emancipatory social change goes against the type of articulation proposed by the state, academia, and political parties.

A first question revolves around the significance of dispersion or fragmentation. What is our vantage point when we use these terms? We are dealing with a perspective that is external, distant, and on top of everything, from above. To speak about a movement, a social subject, or a society as fragmented, does this not imply perceiving it within a state-centered logic, one that presupposes the unity-homogeneity of the social realm and thus its subjects? Moreover, to be a subject supposes some degree of unity or at least non-fragmentation. Supposedly the state-party-academic perspective already knows the role of subjects and can even define when they exist and when they do not.

Secondly, proponents of the articulation of the movements—who are generally those with a state-centric policy—leave to the side the need to take stock of the past one hundred years of socialism and the labor movement. That accounting can be summarized like this: "A controlled and organized transition tends to involve some continuity of exploitation."[61] Again, it is not a theory but just a reading of one hundred years of socialism. However, the left and the academics assure us that without articulation there is not the slightest chance of victory, or the triumphs are merely ephemeral, and that a disarticulated and fragmented movement marches toward certain defeat. Was it not the unification and centralization of past movements that

----

61   Immanuel Wallerstein, *"Marx y el subdesarrollo,"* in *Impensar las ciencias sociales* (México: Siglo XXI, 1998), 186.

enabled the state and capital to neutralize or domesticate them? On the other hand, how can the popular uprisings in Latin America be explained, at least since the Caracazo of 1989, which garnered very significant victories and yet were not convened by formal and established structures?

In El Alto, the distinction between leaders and led is a first and most elemental separation. Without it, there would be no FE-JUVE or COR or any articulation of the social movement. However, in some spaces, such as the rural communities, there are mechanisms to prevent the state realizing itself or the separation between "to lead by obeying" and "to lead by commanding." This is not how it is in the city, but it could be. The Aymara rural communities suffered co-optation and state interference during the long period from 1952 to the 1980s at least. They waged a prolonged internal struggle in order to make what they have today: autonomous organizations. This was not given to them, and it is a construction that other movements and social sectors can produce as well. In this construction, resolving the problem of leadership is key. Leaders must adopt the ways of the elite—not only the manners but also the forms of relating—because as leaders, they must be faithful to the state as well as their bases. Without state loyalty, their role as leaders would be very limited, at least in spaces like large cities.

We have seen that the separation (inside the movement) intensifies with demobilization since it implies impotence, the moment in which the movement-disengagement reaches its limits and then the movement-institution wagers on reining in the leaders. But talking of leaders supposes going into the field of representation. For Weber, everything related to representation goes into the chapter "types of domination" and he insists that representation implies the absence of solidarity. For "below" the FEJUVE and the neighborhood councils, there is a large tapestry, a true society in movement that is what we call the social movement. The panorama presented by the El Alto society is one of a pendulum swinging between dispersion and regrouping, disintegration and unification. We can understand it as struggle, although not necessarily a struggle in the classic sense but rather a fight to encode/decode flows, or social relations in movement.

The El Alto social movement appears to have gone through three stages: from the re-democratization in 1982 until the end of that decade, the 1990s dominated by CONDEPA, and the changes that occurred from the late '90s with the neoliberal crisis and that of CONDEPA. We recall that in the late '80s, "the relative isolation of the neighborhood council with respect to its base" was emphasized.[62] Then came a period of heavy clientelism and co-optation of leaders

---

62   Sandóval and Sostres, *La ciudad prometida, ibid.*, 81.

and, more recently, a contradictory democratization that integrated past practices. From below, it is more complex: there are simultaneous growing pressures and forces and growing trends pushing the grassroots to move away from their own organizations. As a result, it is difficult to identify a linear process, as tendencies and counter-tendencies manifest themselves simultaneously, and practices of grassroots control and the expansion of democracy coexist with forces that reinforce hierarchies and shutter participation.

Typically, analyses of the process experienced by a social movement emphasize its cumulative growth. But if we see it from another place, let's say from the perspective of the movement-disengagement and simultaneously from the longterm, we must discard the concept of accumulation and also the process of development. Instead, we see a pendulum or cyclical movement in which the society in movement and the barrio communities deploy their dispersion capacities on the state/institutional realms and, simultaneously, are constrained by the "cold monster" of the state (to cite Clastres), which seeks at every turn and in every corner of the Aymara world to be born "whole and in one piece." Each step in the expansion of communitarian relations between neighbors represents a decrease in the power of the institutions and of the autonomy of the representatives. The history of the El Alto social movement can be framed in the context of this pendulum dynamic, in which space-time is a productive force of the state and the non-state. There is growth in this cyclical process, which we could call natural, without external objectives.

This dynamic is visible in the fight for public spaces. The state seeks to set its own space-time and, to do so, it is necessary to deconstruct the space-time of society in movement. As the flow of the movements deconstructs state domination, the same happens in reverse. A clash of flows occurs, spreading throughout society. The attempt to legislate the grassroots territorial organizations[63] is just one of them. What happened to the plazas—important spaces for daily socialization and for the coordination of the rebellion—is a good example. La Ceja, the small plaza where book and pamphlet stalls were set up, was fenced off after the movement of May–June 2005. There was an attempt to prevent that space from being used by

---

63   Translator's note: During the implementation of the 1994 Law of Popular Participation (LPP) nongovernmental organizations (NGOs) assumed a new role as intermediaries between the government and the Bolivian population. The law, at the heart of a decentralization program, transferred twenty percent of the national budget to municipalities, established participatory planning, and mandated oversight by grassroots territorial organizations.

young people and other residents for discussions and gatherings.[64] In El Alto, the plazas — which had been built by the residents, used as commercial trade centers, and spaces for meetings, assemblies, and symbolic exchanges — have now become somewhat homogenous thanks to state interference:

> Now what happens is that there is a messed-up policy that means they are starting to enclose the plazas for security reasons. It is also space for parties, and adults misunderstood it. The metal bars they have erected are absurd because they take away the places for gatherings. The plaza is a cultural thing. There is a model of the plaza and the people asked for a plaza and they have been cheated by this the model — it is a state model. The kiosk idea is Spanish; it is what you see in the villages. But here, many plazas are a mere homage to cement, to the wind, to the cold; there is no warmth at all. The mayor's office is offering nothing more than a modernist logic with these kind of trees and cement and not returning to the aesthetic of the cobblestone streets and cacti like in the villages, which is another aesthetic altogether, not of the modern sort, and it just creates more problems than solutions for us. Before there was no flooding; now those living in the South are flooded. The resident suffers because of this imposition of modernity.[65]

The image is of a permanent space-time dispute between movements/communities and the state/political parties: the latter to create division, to divide power, to co-opt, to dominate and consolidate its hegemony; the former, to deconstruct dominance, to re-unite and prevent separation. One way to avoid co-optation is to advocate fragmentation and dispersal, rather than advocating large movements or institutions, thus enabling the movement to acquire spaces of autonomy — gaps through which they can resist, because the state/ party system does not enter into these gaps. When the FEJUVE leaders criticize the grassroots for their "indifference," we are witnessing a silent struggle to avoid subordination.

It should be added, following Foucault, that this struggle between two poles is not one of an exteriority relationship but rather

---

64 Something very similar happened in Buenos Aires: the state installed fences and gates in the main plazas, where the neighborhood assemblies had met after the insurrection of December 2001 — installing exhibitions, holding meetings, sports, and other group activities — because they are the spaces of socialization for the neighbors, and so it was necessary for the state to control them.

65 Interview with Marco Quispe.

that the party/state logic lives in the bosom of the community and the movement; it permeates them, not as something that comes from the outside but rather something that exists in an immanent relationship, as "manifold relationships of force that take shape and come into play in the machinery of production — in families, limited groups, and institutions — are the basis for wide-ranging effects of cleavage that run through the social body as a whole."[66]

66   Michel Foucault, *Historia de la sexualidad*, tomo I (México: Siglo XXI, 1996), 114–115.

CHAPTER 5

Community Justice and El Alto Justice

It seems impossible to travel on the streets of El Alto without coming across hanging dolls. Whether in the main avenues or the more secluded and quiet neighborhood streets, the figures are testament to a peculiarity that distinguishes the Aymara city. Some display posters ("Death to thieves," for example), but most of the dolls made and hung by the residents simply have their heads turned sideways, simulating death by beheading. Others are covered in red paint symbolizing blood, signifying punishment and death. "The hanging dolls mean that here is a house that has been robbed."[1] But at the same time they deliver a warning to thieves, saying:

> The people who live on these streets have come together and have decided that when they catch a thief they are going to kill him." In short, the neighbors are organized, they have their own system of vigilance, like their warning whistles to summon people to defend the district or any affected family. The hanging doll symbolizes the local self-defense organization. In some cases, when residents catch thieves in the act or identify culprits, they have killed them. Some people speak of up to 900 such deaths per year in the city of El Alto, though surely that figure is exaggerated.

The existence of thousands of ominous hanging dolls is a symptom of a powerful territorially based local organization and it seems clear that this form of collective self-defense "is based on communal justice."[2] Or, to put it differently, it is one more urban manifestation of Aymara society, albeit somewhat different—because while community justice seeks, as we shall see, to reintegrate the criminal back into the community, in El Alto they seek to identify the culprit in order to eliminate him.

This chapter does not attempt to judge community justice, or even this form of "justice" applied by the El Alto residents, but

---

1 Testimony of Rosario Adrián of Mujeres Creando in *Mal de Altura* (Buenos Aires: Colectivo Situaciones, 2005).

2 Ibid.

simply to demonstrate that in the Aymara world there are non-state forms of justice. What happens in El Alto is related to the specifics of this highly conflictive city as much or even more so than to Aymara culture generally. Certainly, the security situation for El Alto residents is difficult. The police do not exist or are an accomplice to the thieves, rapists, and those who attack the residents, and state justice is a bad joke. The extreme conditions in El Alto or, to put it more aptly, the extreme conditions of state abandonment and the extreme violence of the mafia-like state apparatus, creates limited solutions. "Here in El Alto the situation gets so out of hand and dangerous that the people become infuriated."[3] Many, like Rosario Adrián, differentiate between community justice and what happens in El Alto. Silvia Rivera feels the same:

> To me, it seems to be a cathartic expression of a profound cultural crisis. Community justice was, in principle, a form of reintegrating the person who had violated the rules. On a third offense, they can kill you. In the best system of justice, the badness of the person is considered, or to put it another way, it is not so much the size of the cow that was stolen but rather the degree of the person's intent to do evil. The seriousness of crime is based on the badness of the person, like if they reveal that they have no desire to change their ways. But there is always a long, considered, and deep period of deliberation. The decision is not taken in the heat of anger. The defendant is allowed to speak; everyone has their say, and that is community justice.[4]

In her view, many of the furious reactions among the people of El Alto city are "a venting of powerlessness, a feeling of insecurity before the state." This situation explains residents' decision to act on their own, based within their experience of community justice, but without the mediation of any collective body because in reality, they do not have the same level of control over the urban spaces as they do in the rural communities.

In any event, it is worth retaining Silvia Rivera's distinction between community justice and the El Alto case. She argues that intimidation is more effective than going to the police, "because state justice is so corrupt that a confessed rapist, or very dangerous guys are just set free." She concludes that what we will refer to as "El Alto justice" is the consequence of a corrupt and morally deteriorated

---

3   Ibid.
4   Interview with Silvia Rivera Cusicanqui.

state judicial apparatus. Furthermore, "it's more dangerous for a local resident to go to the state court for justice because the criminal will come back looking for revenge. El Alto residents' experience in the official courts has been awful."[5]

"We can't understand this form of killing, of taking life," says Rosario Adrián. She maintains that the system of justice practiced in the communities requires its own time and space, in the sense that "the whole community comes together, meets and discusses, enters into dialogue, and asks questions. And finally they arrive at an agreement."[6] According to Silvia Rivera, community justice typically first involves delivering a warning and even a threat to the culprit in order to prevent a relapse, but the situation is just the opposite in El Alto:

> In El Alto it is a reverse process, coming from a lot of experience of ordinary state justice (unlike in the rural communities where there had been no state), and this bad experience made the ordinary justice system illegitimate in the eyes of the residents. The criminals would be taken out of circulation for a while and then they would return and the rumors would abound that these dangerous people had been released in collusion with the police. From that sense of danger, cathartic emotions emerge. There is no mediation process or conditions for which the punishment is progressive in the El Alto system of community justice. The residents kill because it is cathartic. The release comes from the emotional force of the process.[7]

"El Alto justice" has two roots, then: one is related to the existence of a "state against society" where some institutions (security, judicial, etc.) simply go to war against the inhabitants, who they perceive as if they were enemies. On the other hand, neighborhood self-defense is part of the same social and cultural context that has allowed the inhabitants of El Alto to build their own city and manage it. And just as they built their own houses, plazas, sports fields, schools, and paved streets, so too they took the issue of security into their own hands: "As there were no police, the residents had to do guard duty at night in their own neighborhoods, using the dolls and the whistles; they assumed responsibility for the whole security strategy."[8]

---

5   Ibid.
6   Testimony of Rosario Adrián of Mujeres Creando in *Mal de Altura*.
7   Interview with Silvia Rivera Cusicanqui.
8   Interview with Marco Quispe.

When talking about the dolls and the security system in El Alto barrios, the lack of studies and the difficulty of finding people willing to openly discuss the issue is striking. We must put ourselves in the place of the people of El Alto. The state not only fails to guarantee a minimum level of security but actually acts against it and in favor of criminals. In such a situation, what should the residents do in their barrios? They could identify the robbers and rapists and then expel them, as in rural communities. But the next day the expelled would return again with the police, seeking revenge and identifying the most active residents or the leaders of the local councils. Death is a drastic option but guarantees anonymity and therefore protects the residents. Community justice cannot function in the same way as the rural communities. The Aymara space-time of the rural communities allows justice to be carried out openly, based on dialogue, with enough time to make reflective decisions based on consensus. In El Alto, the inhabitants can convene a barrio assembly but they cannot prevent the infiltration of police or accomplices of the criminal, rendering the neighborhood council and the residents vulnerable to reprisals.

There is no question that this form of "El Alto justice" is too drastic and does not allow for any forms of intermediation. Hence, the need to highlight the foundational mechanisms upon which rural community justice functions, which may in time come to fruition in the cities, the centers of state and elite power and domination.

A Non-state Justice

Justice and law are social relations. And just as the state must be understood as a social relationship—that is, as a relationship between human beings—we must "understand the law as a social relation, in the same sense that Marx described capital as a social relationship."[9] In other words, "the *regulation* of social relations under certain conditions *assumes a legal character*."[10] You can even establish an analogy between commodity fetishism, as Evgeni Pashukanis does, and a legal fetishism—in both cases the relations between human beings appear as relations between things or, in this case, between "legal subjects:"

At a certain stage of development, therefore, human relations in the production process assume a double and enigmatic form. In one sense, they operate as a relation-

9   Evgeni Pashukanis, *Teoría general del derecho y marxismo* (Barcelona: Labor, 1976).

10   Ibid., 65, emphasis in the original.

ship between things/commodities; and in another sense, on the contrary, as mutual relations between reciprocal independent and equal subjects. Next to the mystical property of value appears something no less enigmatic: the law. At the same time, a single, unitary relationship takes on two fundamental abstract aspects: one economic and one legal.[11]

The abstract concept of a legal subject, which turns people into bearers of rights, is a reflection of the "abstract and impersonal power of the state."[12] With the development of bourgeois social relations, the abstract nature of law appeared, because "every man becomes a man in general, all work is social work in general, and each subject becomes an abstract legal subject," and because the will of the legal subject "has its real foundation in the desire to alienate acquiring and to acquire alienating."[13]

We reach the point where "the process of constituting legal categories loses its 'naturalness,' transforming into a form of capitalist mystification of the circulation and the reproduction of capital, as an extension and deepening of exploitation."[14] From this point of view, it is easily understood that both the law and the state are forms of capitalist social relations."[15] And, therefore, they are not valid outside of that context. Similarly we cannot speak strictly of an "Aymara state" — in societies in which capitalism and the state are not consolidated realities — nor can we talk of justice or community law.

• • • • • • • • • • • •

Community justice should be understood as a set of cultural practices of indigenous peoples who seek to overcome their conflicts in order to maintain the continuity of their communities. As we have seen, the term "justice" is misleading and we should find another.[16] In effect, the concept of justice refers to a statist relation. The law has been defined as an order "externally guaranteed by the probability of *coercion* (physical or mental) carried out by *a team of individuals* instituted with the mission of compelling the enforcement of that order or punishing its transgression."[17]

---

11   Ibid., 99.

12   Ibid.,100.

13   Ibid.,101–102.

14   Antonio Negri, *La forma-Estado* (Madrid: Akal, 2003), 263.

15   John Holloway, *Cambiar el mundo sin tomar el poder* (Buenos Aires: Herramienta, 2002), 120.

16   Enrique Mier Cueto, *Las prácticas jurídicas aymaras desde una perspectiva cultural* (Sucre: Poder Judicial, 2005), 61.

17   Max Weber, *Economía y sociedad*, 27. Italics in the original.

The existence of a team of people imposing justice from outside is what distinguishes the practice of law, which is a standard
"not externally guaranteed."[18] In the case of the communities, there is
no such separation because it is the community itself imparting justice, whether it is the authorities, or the communal assembly. Hence,
strictly speaking, there is no talk of law or justice but of cultural
practices to resolve conflicts and ensure internal balance. This mechanism of healing or "system of conflict resolution" is closely linked to
the process of legitimization of the authorities, and this requires the
presence of a "third party" that has legitimacy and socially accepted
power.[19] The difference is that this "third party" is not a "team" or
external, separate institution placed above society, but rather constituted by the community itself and its own authorities. Therefore,
for community justice to function, the community needs to be able to
legitimately choose its own authorities.

At one time or another, all decisions in Aymara communities
pass through the communal assembly, whether because the authorities responsible for resolving conflicts have been elected by the communal assembly or because, if these authorities are incompetent, the
assembly has the final word. What we find is "a collective that ad-
ministers justice" and "its members are part of the tribunal as prosecution and defense witnesses until the fairest solution is reached,"
because "all members of the community know the norms and existing legal principles.[20]

The community sanctions that are applied meet three, interre-
lated conditions: moral, social, and legal sanctions, which are united
in the prosecution of a crime. Four parts or steps are mentioned in
resolving a conflict: an outline of the conflict by the authority (elected
authorities or the assembly); the introduction of the background and
actions to prove the facts; "long deliberations between the different
parties" including the authorities; and finally, "the agreement" based
on consensus, which is an essential and lauded component.[21]

In any event, before taking any decision regarding the penalties (in the Aymara case: moral sanction, community work, a fine in
cash or kind, whipping, exile, or death penalty), debates occur and
it takes a while to process the conflict. The sanction seeks reparation above punishment and reconciliation between the parties before
causing any separation in the community. Nevertheless, community

---

18   Ibid., 25.

19   Enrique Mier Cueto, *Las prácticas jurídicas aymaras desde una perspectiva cultural*, 66.

20   Marcelo Fernández, *La ley del ayllu* (La Paz: Pieb, 2004), 54.

21   Enrique Mier Cueto, *Las prácticas jurídicas aymaras desde una perspectiva cultural*, 73–74.

justice has been changing: previously, there were no economic penalties, and sometimes now the punishment is to refer the case to the
state justice system. The aim is, wherever possible, to reintegrate
the person who has committed a violation back into the community. Hence the importance of reparation and the ritual, because they
believe the "unlawful not only disturbs human order, but also the
divine."[22]

For Silvia Rivera, the death penalty is exceptional and rarely
applied, and if it does take place, the offender accepts the outcome as
an acknowledgment of his guilt: "The entire community takes things
in stride. They are consulted, to see if the decision is correct or not.
It is very common that the guilty party will be pardoned, but in some
cases the process reaches a level of recognition and the criminal com-
mits suicide. He suffers greatly and often breaks under the psycho-
logical pressure."[23]

According to Marcelo Fernández, in the Aymara cosmovision,
justice is part of the *suma qamana*, meaning "the good way of life,"
or rebirth, renewal and revival; a way "to live fully and reciprocally
with other elements or lives that surround the persons and societies,
experience, (self-)confidence, and (self-)respect being the most important elements."[24] Therefore, one cannot deal with the community
system of resolving conflicts from a Western point of view as if it
were a legal system, since there is no separation between the political and legal authorities, nor between "the real legal world and the
cosmic ritual-religious law."[25] The differences between state justice
and the law of the *ayllu* can be summarized as follows:

> The paradigms of positive state law is characterized by
> the "separation of discourse and the social body," the
> rupture between the present and the past, and especially
> the division between law and justice—that is to say, the
> values of the practice. Conversely, the reality of Indian
> justice is conducted by the standards of the past; law and
> justice walk hand-in-hand, constituting an indissoluble
> unity. In other words, the memory of the "souls" governs
> the present, represented by *yatiri*, forming part of the
> structure of the original authorities, who exercise their
> functions in a logic of lending their service according to
> the road or *thaki*.[26]

---

22   Ibid., 79.
23   Interview with Silvia Rivera Cusicanqui.
24   Marcelo Fernández, *La ley del ayllu*. Preface to the second edition.
25   Ibid., 332.
26   Ibid., 337.

The community system of conflict resolution has some important characteristics from the standpoint of emancipation—that is,
characteristics that have value beyond their own communities. It is
an *autonomous* system, disengaged from the state, even if colonialism
has embedded some norms of the state judiciary in it (the records
and economic penalties, among others). It is an *integral* system that is
built on totally different values that are often antagonistic to the state
judiciary. The purpose of this system is to maintain internal stability
and thus ensure the continuity of Indian society.

Secondly, unlike universalized state law, community justice is
a practice characterized by *the local, temporal, and spatial,* "strongly
depending on the characteristics of the social context from which it
arises."[27] It is worth repeating that this is not a system of law or an alternative system of justice, but a manifestation of another reality that
does not necessitate comparison with the Western legal system. It is
a system for resolving conflicts based on a culture and a cosmovision
different from the West.

Thirdly, we are dealing with a *non-state* system of conflict resolution. The non-statism is evident in the absence of a specialized
body (a "team" in Weber's words), separated from society, in charge
of implementing justice. The non-separation, a basic feature of the
Aymara world, means that responsibility for resolving conflicts lies
in the hands of the community itself and its own authorities. But
the concept of non-separation has another possible reading, related
to the integral nature that I have already referred to—it does not
separate the present from the past, nor values from their implementation, nor the crime from its context, nor the real world from the
sacred and religious world. This is because what is sought is not punishment, and therefore separation, but to recover balance through
compromise—which is among the most important legal principles of
community—as a way to restore harmony.

This form of non-state conflict resolution is itself dispersed and
a dispersing agent, as well as decentralized. As we have seen, it is
not an appeal to an abstract and universal law and there is not a
homogeneous, judicial subject. In different communities, there are
different punishments for the same crime. There is no single model
or paradigm that applies in all cases and places. Similarly, there is no
single, centralized body in a position to resolve conflicts, but there is
a series of "authorities" in charge of dealing with them, according to
the specific characteristics of the conflict, running from the family to
the community assembly, passing through the various authorities. In
sum, there is no one model of justice or specialized body in charge of

---

27 Enrique Mier Cueto, *Las prácticas jurídicas aymaras desde una perspectiva cultural,* 62.

imparting it, but rather a diversity of instances and a multiplicity of possible solutions, because "Indian law is the sum of pluralities."[28]

However, the Aymara form of conflict resolution includes oppression and servitude as well as non-state and emancipatory aspects: for example, the penalty for adultery is punishment with whips. These measures are not only shocking to those who live in Westernized societies, even in Latin America, but also from the viewpoint of the oppression of women, children, and youth. In this case, the community very clearly forms a part of the chain of constraints and restraints that always harm the weakest and hinder individual growth. You do not need to be an advocate of individualism and universalism to recognize the oppressive aspects of some community practices. It is thus heartening that the Zapatista women have pointed out the need to "distinguish between the customs that are good from those that are bad."[29]

On the other hand, the colonial system forced the Indian system of conflict resolution underground. In this respect, the fate of the system of community justice has traveled the same trajectory as that of the plight of the previously semi-clandestine existence of community authorities: a long journey from concealment in order to protect the traditions, towards, particularly in recent decades, a slow emergence into public light. Despite being clandestine, the legitimacy of community justice is further ratified by the ineffectiveness and corruption of state justice. A key point is the application of sanctions, in particular the heavy penalties, which had to have been "hidden from the state and the view of the communities themselves to prevent the reprisals that might be raised against them."[30]

At this point, it is advisable to return to the El Alto experience. As we have seen, some conflicts are resolved by the neighborhood councils and trade unions: quarrels, disputes between neighbors, faults with the organization, etc. In these cases there seems to be a system of conflict resolution inspired by community practices. The case of the hanging dolls is different. This is more a method of self-defense, albeit rudimentary, than a form of community justice. There is no doubt that the neighborhood community should defend itself since nobody else is going to do so. And it seems very positive that they defend themselves without creating a specialized, separate apparatus, just as they do not create a specialized apparatus to mobilize and fight for their interests. Nevertheless, this issue deserves deeper discussion, and requires the capacity to grasp without prejudice or compromise practices that should not be justified by state hostility or dangerous situations.

---

28   Marcelo Fernández, *La ley del ayllu*, 345.

29   Guiomar Rovira, *Mujeres de maíz* (México: Era, 1997), 172.

30   Marcelo Fernández, *La ley del ayllu*, 108.

CHAPTER 6

Toward an Aymara "State"?

The Achacachi Manifesto, issued on April 9, 2001, should be read from the last page: dozens of communities, stamps, or those of sub-centrals and agricultural unions; more than eighty signatures of representatives of thousands of community members and their families in the province of Omasuyos. The pages where the stamps appear can be viewed like a community jigsaw puzzle or, if you prefer, as the social fabric of one of the eight El Alto urban districts composed of dozens of neighborhoods, villas, and communities. This complex articulation of units, irreconcilable in their differences, can only be described as "united" by ignoring the careful preservation of each of their distinct characteristics, which are only united at certain "very critical" times, as the Manifesto itself points out in its first paragraph. So, we can begin to understand what an Aymara "state" would be like—or, a horizontal articulation of powers not separated from their communities—starting from this juxtaposition of community stamps.

Each of the stamps, printed by the president or the secretary of the community, is much more than the signature of the representative: it is the collective expression of the concept of "to lead obeying," and behind these seals are dozens of meetings, assemblies, consultations, and debates. But, above all, this is how these dozens of communities articulate themselves. This is the basic form of what, for lack of a better word, we will call an "Aymara state" or the articulation imagined and constructed by the Aymara during the deployment of their potency as a society.

The stamps appear next to each other, without hierarchies or synthesis, and yet the seal of the central province—the most "important" according to Western logic—would not have even the smallest value in the absence of the other stamps, the seals of all the provincial communities—or at least a significant number of them. This consensus of horizontal seals, this rainbow of stamps/communities, could be seen as an expression of Aymara society in movement (like a non-state in session without representatives).

The articulation of communities that produced the Manifesto of Achacachi is a temporal confluence, which occurred in order to produce something—in this case a document, and in others a mobilization or a set of actions decided upon by the communities. The articulation (or state, if you wish) only makes sense as a mechanism for overseeing a collective decision, for giving form to "leading by obeying." It is not an institution, nor even a permanent or fixed body, but rather a temporary, mobile one. It is an unstable articulation. It is a matter of thinking, in the social field, about the possibility of an articulation capable of combining the stability of the structure with the fluidity of change, something Prigogine defines as "dissipative structures," which are the union between stillness and movement, time suspended and time in flux.[1]

In the social field, "dissipative structures" appear in small groups of youth, women, and others, and can be viewed as areas where there is an unstable equilibrium.[2] However, the existence of larger spaces of "dissipative structures"—covering hundreds of thousands of people and entire regions, bringing together the contradictory characteristics of stability and change, order and dissipation— seems a challenge, and remains far off, if it is possible at all.

The Idea of State-power Among the Aymaras

In 1970, Fausto Reinaga published *The Indian Revolution* that included the Manifesto of the Bolivian Indian Party.[3] The question of the state and the organization of Aymara power had little relevance in it. The work defends the "struggle for the conquest of power—the Power to build a new society."[4] When addressing the issue of the Indian revolution, it argues that the Indian conquest of power is "for the establishment of socialism."[5] On the state, it says: "The state shall be a power, and the nation a community of blood and spirituality; a unity of flesh and soul."[6] Inspired by *The Communist Manifesto*, it makes a

---

1   Ilya Prigogine and Isabelle Stengers, *La nueva alianza, Metamorfosis de la ciencia* (Madrid: Alianza, 1990). According to Prigogine the dissipative structures are islands of order in a sea of chaos, but that order emerges spontaneously and is maintained at a steady state far from equilibrium. See also Fritjof Capra, *La trama de la vida* (Barcelona: Anagrama, 1998), 193–205.

2   Raúl Zibechi, *La revuelta juvenil de los 90* (Montevideo: Nordan, 1997) and *Genealogía de la revuelta* (La Plata: Letra Libre, 2003).

3   Fausto Reinaga, *La revolución india* (La Paz: Fundación Amáutica Fausto Reinaga, 2001).

4   Ibid., 386–387.

5   Ibid., 443.

6   Ibid., 446.

fervent appeal for the unity of Indians: "Indians of Bolivia, unite!" "Unity will lead us to Power," it says.[7]

Beyond a vague appeal to the past, Qullasuyu,[8] and Tawantinsuyu, Reinaga is not clear whether there is any difference between the existing capitalist state and Reinaga's proposed Aymara state. In the introduction to his book *Tesis India*, published in 1971, Guillermo Carnero Hoke, "leader of Peruvian Communal Power," said that Indian power "derives from the word 'community.' Knowing how an Inka community functions is to have an ethnic government in hand."[9] He posits the need to return to community organization and concludes: "The great Confederation of Communities—that is the Indian Government, that is Indian Power, that is Indian Socialism!"[10]

Reinaga's theory of revolution tends to reflect Marx, but it should not be assumed that his theory of the state has been copied from Marx entirely. In any case, we should note that he offers no clear definition of what an Indian state would be like. This absence is not accidental. In the same period (1973), a group of Aymara residents in La Paz passed around the Tiwanaku Manifesto, which was "the most successful synthesis so far of the various currents that comprise the Katarist movement."[11] The document, signed by the Centro Campesino Tupak Katari, MINK'A, the Association of Peasant Teachers, and the Association of Peasant Students of Bolivia, made no reference to what an Aymara state would be like. It only states that "economic and political power is the foundation of cultural liberation."[12] At that time, what would later became the powerful Aymara movement was in its infancy.

And in a later phase of the movement, in 1990 specifically, Felipe Quispe published the book *Tupak Katari Lives and Returns ... Dammit*, in which he offered his own vision of the "Tupac Katari" revolution. In the conclusion, he argued for the need to resume the armed struggle so as to unleash the "Indian Community Revolution"

---

7   Ibid., 447.

8   Translator's note: Qullasuyu was a provincial region of the Inca Empire. It related specifically to the Aymara territories which are now largely incorporated into the modern South American states of Bolivia, Chile, Peru and Argentina. Recently, there has been moves to form a "Greater Qullasuyu" (or Qullana Suyu Marka) which would incorporate a territory similar to the former Inca Empire, known as Tawantinsuyu in Quechua.

9   Fausto Reinaga, *Tesis India* (La Paz: Hilda Reinaga, 2003), 14.

10   Ibid., 15.

11   Silvia Rivera Cusicanqui, "Luchas campesinas contemporáneas en Bolivia: el movimiento 'katarista': 1970–1980" in René Zavaleta Mercado (ed.) *Bolivia hoy* (México: Siglo XXI, 1983), 142.

12   Javier Hurtado, *El Katarismo* (La Paz: Hisbol, 1986), 304.

to achieve self-determination for the original nations, destroying capitalism:

> [A]nd upon these ruins to construct and return to the Aymara Commune, and to form a Union of Socialist Nations of Qullasuyu, creating a society without class and race, where the Collectivism and Communitarianism of the *ayllus* reign, where we shall be the owners of our ancestral Pacha Mama, of our own destiny and political power, so that the Aymaras can govern ourselves in the time of Tiwanakense.[13]

That same year the Katarist Liberation Movement issued a pamphlet entitled *The Social Model of the Ayllu*, which examines in detail how an Aymara society of the future might look. The text advocates for an updated reconstruction of the *ayllu* that would not just be a return to the situation before the Conquest. The forms of organization of the *ayllu* would be based on four types of social relations of work: *Ayni* (cooperation between families of the *ayllu*), *Mink'a* (reciprocity between *ayllus*), *mit'a* (reciprocity between *ayllus* and the *marka*[14]), and *q'amaña* (environmental reciprocity).[15]

The political practice of the *ayllu* (designated authorities by rotation and in succession for a limited time, to ensure no monopoly of power) is the basis of political power. The pamphlet points out that "politics are not only exercised at *ayllu* level, but are more widespread at the *marka* level through to the traditional authorities known as *mallkus*, which in turn are appointed by the different *ayllus*, rotated and in succession."[16] It is about building a "communal society" based on the *ayllu*, from the bottom up, including the formation of communally based businesses "to build the great Economic and Political Confederation of *Ayllus* and Communities, where the *jilakatas* and *mallkus*, the traditionally appointed leaders, are the authorities of this new social and economic model."[17] These authorities would govern through mass meetings and assemblies.

At the beginning of the new century, some of these ideas were embodied in the powerful mobilizations of the peasant farmers' movement. The Achacachi Manifesto was issued on April 9, 2001, dur-

---

13   Felipe Qhispi Wanka, *Tupak Katari vive y vuelve...carajo* (La Paz: Ofensiva Roja, 1990), 313–314.

14   Translator's note: *marka* is a set of *ayllus*, or the territory of the community.

15   Movimiento Katarista de Liberación, *Modelo social del ayllu. Pensamiento katarista* (La Paz: MKL, 1990), 6.

16   Ibid., 8.

17   Ibid., 28.

ing the full mobilization of the Aymara communities of the Altiplano against the government, preceded by the Charter for Rebuilding the Aymara-Quichwa Nation. Six months earlier, amid a formidable Aymara mobilization on October 6, 2000, the Omasuyos trade union leaders of cantons, centrals, and sub-centrals stamped more than forty seals on the Declaration of Achacachi, representing organizations from six provinces of North La Paz, agreeing to unity of action.

This series of documents, resolutions, and manifestos were produced under very special circumstances: the first three major Aymara uprisings of the twentieth century, whose epicenter was the province of Omasuyos and the city of Achacachi—a historical, economic, political, and cultural Aymara center. In April 2000, the first uprising against the water law took place, which lasted nine days, with widespread road blockades. It began in the Omasuyos province but had effects nationwide. A movement of this magnitude had not been seen since 1979, during the struggle against the dictatorship. It made extensive use of the system of taking turns and rotation to ensure the blockades were maintained, using mass meetings and assemblies as a means of decision making (up to 15,000 Aymara are concentrated in Achacachi). The government declared martial law, but the police disobeyed, leading to a mutiny. This cumulated on April 9, with the invasion of Achacachi by two thousand soldiers from the Anti-aircraft Artillery Group, arriving in twenty trucks to militarize the city, and surrounding communities. The military killed two youth and the public responded by confronting the army, killing a captain and destroying the municipal prefecture, the police precinct, and the prison, freeing the prisoners. "It was the first major defeat of the prevailing neoliberal system in Bolivia,"[18] which happened simultaneously with the "water war" being waged in Cochabamba, in a struggle where the Aymara "brought the *community ethos* into play as a strategy of struggle."[19]

Shortly afterward, a new uprising—the second—began in September and October of 2000, covering the entire Altiplano region and the north valley of La Paz. The most notable feat during the nineteen days of this uprising was establishing the "indigenous general headquarters of Qalachaka," which became the nerve center of the movement. Here 50,000 militarized communards congregate, exercising self-government in deed. This movement, which continues and grows, represents a long-term shift in the forms and objectives of the indigenous movement:

---

18   Pablo Mamani Ramírez, *Geopolíticas Indígenas* (El Alto, Cades, 2005), 95.

19   Félix Patzi, "Rebelión indígena contra la colonialidad y la transnacionalización de la economía: triunfos y vicisitudes del movimiento indígena desde 2000 a 2003" in *Ya es otro tiempo el presente* (La Paz: Muela del Diablo, 2003), 208.

Unlike what happened in 1979, the aims of this movement were not to defend representative democracy or to
win limited demands. On the contrary, it signified, firstly, the beginning of the end of representative democracy
and the collapse of the neoliberal economic model implemented in 1985 and thereafter. And secondly, it was the
beginning of the legitimization of the original nations
confederation's political project for self-determination.[20]

The Declaration of Achacachi was issued at this particular political conjuncture. The document has six points; its first calls for
"the revival of indigenous power and of the original nations of this
republic dominated by economic, political, and ideological power as
a legacy of colonialism." The third point represents a qualitative leap
in the history of recent Aymara struggles: "For any joint action of the
peasant movement, the general headquarters and capital of Indigenous power will be located at Achacachi, Omasuyos province, department of La Paz." The fifth point reads: "The original nations will
respond to any action against the peasants by taking up arms." And
the sixth: "To establish Councils of Communal Justice in the indigenous territories instead of magistrates and police. Also, to expel the
repressive bodies of the government, the police, and the army."[21]

The third uprising took place in June and July 2001, lasting
about two months and also encompassing the Altiplano and valleys
north of La Paz. During this movement, alongside the "General
staff" of the Qalachaka, several micro headquarters were created to
control Aymara territory, and others were created that were mobile,
sporadic, and diffused.[22] A "civil war" was declared and "an Indian
state of siege." In this social atmosphere, shortly before on April 7,
commemorating the anniversary of the events of the previous year,
the Charter for the Reconstruction of the Aymara-Quichwa Nation
was issued. The document was received by a massive concentration
"of the children of Mallku Qhapaq and Mama Ajlla" and offered
in the memory of Tupak Katari and other historical revolutionary
figures. "Bolivia was established on top of our millennium-old Qyul-
lana or Qullasuyu," it asserts, and "the clandestine government of the
Aymara has maintained its political and social institutions." The text
goes further in stating that "we are living a new historical era with
an autonomous government, because we liberated ourselves in 2000
from the sub-prefecture, the police, and other repressive, thieving,

---

20   Ibid., 215.

21   *Declaración de Achacachi*, Achacachi, 6 October, 2000. Emphasis in the original.

22   Pablo Mamani Ramírez, *Geopolíticas indígenas*, 97.

and corrupt forms of the government of the Republic." The charter calls for rebuilding the political and administrative unit, which was known as Omasuyos, the Jach'a Umasuyu, which "will be in concert" with other similar units and will contain an "autonomous government of the Aymara" situated within the *ayllu* economy and its institutions." The original transcript of the document states—although this does not appear in the final version—that the government "will be formed by two representatives of each provincial town, which will meet in the Ulaqa [Parliament or Congress]."[23]

The Manifesto of Achacachi, delivered on the same day, does not go any further although it does present a detailed list of the problems of the Aymara and Quechua people as well as their history and recent events of note. "The restoration of the Qullasuyu as a model of a nation-state" is the only reference in these documents as to what an Aymara state might look like. Three months later, on July 7, 2001, with the region fully militarized, the Aymara Supreme Council issued a statement denouncing the repression and appealing to the Aymara to expand the struggle. The statement points out that "Bolivia is not a solution to our problems." The communities of Omasuyos and the North of La Paz appear increasingly to be outside of the Bolivian state.

Thus far we have looked at the documents related to the social movement. At no point does it seems clear that the Aymara are defending the idea of founding a state, perhaps because, as Patzi says, "The Indians and workers are not rooted in a statist vision."[24] It seems clear that the logic of the state is not part of their historical learning process or their cosmovision, beyond the brief and confusing passage in the Achacachi Manifesto referring to a "model of nation-state." There is a strong consensus that the community *ayllus* would be the basis for a desirable society, and that there would be some form of regional coordination of communities, which in the recent documents was referred to as *Jach'as*, and that would be the basic territorial unit grouping together various communities. Apart from this formulation, nothing clear is indicated, beyond the desire for the Bolivian state to disappear.

In fact, the general headquarters of Qalachaka is perhaps the most revealing indicator of the Aymara vision of power—one that is not split from the community, a non-state power.

---

23 *Acta de reconstitución del Gobierno de la Nación Aymara-Quichwa.* Capital Achakachi del Milenario Umasuyu, Achacachi, 9th April 2001.

24 Félix Patzi, ibid., 222.

Diffused Powers; Centralized Powers

"For me the state is an instance of coordination," says Patzi. He is referring, of course, to what an Indian state could be like. But immediately the contradiction between an Aymara and Bolivian nation appears:

> It is impossible to think of a communal system without a nation. I do not agree with the modern national fragmentations, but we must take the national creations as a reality. In Bolivia there will be the Bolivian revolution. You cannot erase nations from history. For this reason, I criticize the idea of Qullasuyo. As a dream it is good but it is not real. "Communards of the world unite" could possibly be, but in a national form.[25]

Notwithstanding his insistence on viewing the state as a "coordinator," he thinks that parliament as a legislative body should disappear because "the community will make the laws," and he notes the difference between "the liberal representative who deliberates and decides" and the community representative "who only expresses and executes what has been decided by the community, a representative who is a transmitter." In his view, "the state should be placed not above but below society, to carry out its decisions, to discuss the expressions of the various communities, but not to supplant them."

A tension appears when determining how to denominate this coordinating organization, since the word "state" refers to a clearly separate reality on top of society. Nevertheless, any instance of coordination can become an elite that is separate from society. "The system of rotation," maintains Patzi, "eliminates this entirely. The danger of creating elites is overcome with the system of rotation." He imagines the presidency as a revolving role: first one department gets its turn and within this department turns are taken, and therefore the same person never assumes presidency more than once and control is with the collective. "Just like how it is done in the community. Everyone will get the opportunity to have a turn," he says. It would only take developing what already exists at a community level, creating a general theory to raise awareness of the process, and expand it.

For his part, Pablo Mamani believes that the term "state" is merely a "semantic loan," because "state is a logic of the centrality of power and we think of a state in the logic of the *ayllu*, territorially and bureaucratically de-concentrated, but with a rotation of government by sectors and regions and parcels."[26] In his view, the

---

25   Interview with Félix Patzi.
26   Interview with Pablo Mamani Ramírez.

key is to overcome centralism and bank on "a kind of multiversity logic." "Diversity comes together in the state," he says, "so that state and society would no longer be separate. The state is the society and society is state." Remember that the word "state" does not exist in Aymara, but the term *suyo* is used, which refers to a great political and territorial region:

> If a revolution triumphed, power would still exist, but as a diffuse power, de-concentrated, cohesive, and not coercive. Armies would be necessary, but armies like the Qalachaka army—one that appears and disappears, that forms in certain moments and then dissolves, to appear again in other conditions and in a different manner, but nevertheless an army that has a real effect, which is to make people obey. The state is society and society is the state. We are talking about a political philosophy very different from that of Weber and Marx. But if we do not have a state, then each will want to have their own micro-state.[27]

Like the texts of the movement, these two Aymara sociologists take the *ayllu* as their starting point. In effect, the Bolivian uprisings beginning April 2000 cannot be understood without emphasizing community organization. Moreover, they form part of the slow rise of communities, and of the social relationships they embody. The *ayllus* have inspired structures of mobilization "based in the original structures." Mobilizations directed by traditional authorities—or, that is to say, councils of government of the *markas* and *ayllus*.[28] The communities have been able to recreate themselves because they are undergoing a long process of change, in which the new role of women, youth in general, and young Aymara professionals in particular, stands out. But at base, they struggle as they do in the communities, combining the concentration/dispersion model, as happened in the October 2001 blockades, when it was used for the first time in a systematic way in shifts by *parcialidades*:[29]

> In these circumstances, they are putting in movement the socio-political structures of the *ayllus*. At night they go from house to house holding small meetings to clarify *ayllu* strategies: that everyone should go out and block-

---

27 Ibid.

28 Pablo Mamani Ramírez, *El rugir de las multitues* (La Paz Yachaywasi, 2004), 73.

29 Translator's note: each *ayllu* has two *parcialidades*: *aransaya* and *urinsaya;* the upper part and the lower part, representing a concept deeply rooted in the Andean cosmovision.

ade "together" but "dispersed." ... Half the members of
each family must stay in their houses to feed the children
and livestock, and to graze cattle, sheep, llamas, and al-
pacas. This means under *ayllu* logic: everybody "separate" and "together" becomes responsible for mobilizing
the *ayllu* forces. That is, half the members of the *ayllus*
are on the roads and the other half are preparing food
and drink to take to the road.[30]

Thus, combining concentration and dispersion, both in the territory of the community spaces and those chosen for the blockade,
the movement achieves unity without unification. In the same way,
based on the knowledge of the *ayllu* and the community social relations, alliances are made between *markas* during the mobilization
without resorting to an apparatus that links the communities, but
through ritual moments of gathering. During these consolidations of
unity, "some arrive with *Wiphala* flags, with coca leaves and a little
alcohol to *chew coca with the Gods*... in these spaces, men and women
coming from different *markas* embrace to keep the *ayllu* movement
united.[31] The strength of the blockades is that they become the space-
time of the internal unification of the *ayllus* and *markas*, without formal structures or apparatus.

Something similar happens with *mallkus y t'allas* (male and female authorities of the *markas*) and the *jilakatas* (the authorities of
the *ayllus*). These political, social, religious, and territorial authorities
become the leaders of the mobilizations despite being formally con-
voked by the union, the peasants' central or sub-central. As Mamani
has noted, this is a new phenomenon that reveals the depth of the
turnaround that is taking place: "During the great Indian uprisings
of the colonial and republic period, the Kataris-Amarus had been
revered figures; now the *Mallkus* have emerged as the new reference for the genealogy of the symbols of indigenous authority and
power."[32]

The decisive factor is that all the enormous potential of the
Aymara movement lies in "the micro-spaces of social life": this set of
social relations manifested in the communities, in the connections between communities, in events and assemblies within the community
authorities.[33] To sum up: this is a society in movement, its hardened
core made of non-capitalist social relations in movement, no longer
depending on external factors to create political scenarios, agendas,

---

30   Pablo Mamani Ramírez, *El rugir de las multitudes*, 80.

31   Ibid., 89.

32   Ibid., 106.

33   Ibid.,183.

and strategies of change. Instead, these circumstances are created on the basis of the maturation of their own internal time and, eventually, expand in a multiplicity of forms. As necessary, the grassroots of this society make some type of articulation possible that is bigger than the *markas*, a kind of state that is not a state but something else, and will be nothing more than the recreating of the *ayllu* and the *marka*, or, that is, the social relations of the community. At this point, Aymara logic indicates that it does not need any articulation, except that which does not cancel and destroy the potencies that form the *ayllu*. Counter-powers only convert themselves into power by deconstructing the very potencies that have allowed them to become counter-powers.

Although they do not prioritize the question of a new Aymara state, Silvia Rivera and Esteban Ticona provide a unique view of the process of "reconstitution of the *ayllu*" and its liberation from the tutelage of the union—or better said, the state—since the 1980s.[34] Ticona reflects with great subtlety upon the so-called "fragmentation" and "factionalism" in the Jesús de Machaca movement, which somehow echoes the lived process of the local councils of El Alto in recent years. He notes that from the revolution of 1952 until the 1980s, there is a level of fragmentation within the grassroots organizations that exceeds that of the population growth, and that each union has a lower number of families than the first syndicates or the older *ayllus*. He concludes that "divisive forces have been more prevalent than unifying ones."[35]

But Ticona breaks with a statist vision and argues that when the division is not the product of an internal conflict, "that which appears as 'factionalism' or subdivision is merely the re-strengthening of the old identity in a new context," and thereby "increases the opportunities for encounter and exchange between all who live there or move in." In effect, communities consist of face-to-face relationships, fluid communication between people, and active participation. These characteristics stop working if the society or the group exceeds a certain mass threshold, thereby making it impossible for "the virtual consensus decision making process in assemblies to function, as well as *thaki* (the way of posts and prestige), rotation, and internal reciprocity."[36]

---

34 María Eugenia Choque and Carlos Mamani, "Reconstitución del Ayllu y derechos de los Pueblos Indígenas: El Movimiento Indio en los Andes de Bolivia." in *Los Andes desde los Andes*, 147–170.

35 Esteban Ticona, *La lucha por el poder comunal. Jesús de Machaqa, la marka rebelde*, vol. 3 (La Paz: Cedoin-Cipca, 1997), 240.

36 Ibid., 241.

This point is closely related to the question of the state, because "in Aymara thought there is no idea that the most valuable attribute is oneness; for them there is unity in otherness," which is why duality better expresses this complementariness and balance. Thus, the process of divisions and subdivisions, the so-called fragmentation, is a strategy of communal resistance against the colonial state, a sort of "re-communalization," which seeks autonomy linked to micro-government and to community and local power. Ticona concludes that this tendency toward diversity is in line with the search for a certain order, which does not exclude the unity of the Aymara people but reinforces it from another place.[37] That other place which is re-constituted is not the same community, but one in which educated young people take the places formerly occupied by only the elderly and adults. In other words, the Aymara world is re-communalizing and transforming itself—we can say it is re-democratizing itself—enabling the participation of sectors previously excluded from decision making. This process not only strengthens the power of the *ayllu* as a space for renewal of the Aymara world without losing its identity, but also deepens its libertarian values and practices.

Meanwhile, Rivera has a complementary, double perspective. On the one hand, she argues that the strength of the self-determination of the mobilizations

> emanates from those micro-networks of interwoven local powers, made up of the assemblies and rural unions, the blockade committees and the neighborhood councils, the guilds and associations. These have a national presence as a dense network of shared ideologies and slogans, where the community/map (masculine vision) is tied to the community/weave (female vision) and creates a new praxis of production and circulation of practical and productive knowledge that is ethical as well as organizational.[38]

This micro view, linked to the long memory, is complemented by its vision of change (the *Pachakutik*), understood as a change in the Aymara social world, in which internal space-time (*manqapacha*) emerges with female participation, the ascension of democracy and the sociability of those on the bottom.[39] "*Pachakutik* is not the taking of power, but the subversion of power—turning the world upside

---

37   Ibid., 244–247.

38   Silvia Rivera Cusicanqui, *Oprimidos pero no vencidos* (La Paz: Aruwiyiri-Yachaywasi, 2003), 27.

39   Silvia Rivera Cusicanqui, "Metáforas y retóricas del levantamiento de octubre," *Bolivian Studies Journal/Revista E*, vol. 4, February 2004.

down. What is inside comes out and what is outside comes in. It is to invert the terms."[40] It is, in her opinion, one way to decolonize power, not beginning from the external (state, parties) but "to decolonize one's own head," —a internal process of renewal.

A substantial part of this process of renewal, perhaps even its core —that which gives internal coherence to the entire itinerary—is the expansion of community logic by dispersion and dissemination throughout the twentieth century, expanding and spreading from the bottom up. The so-called "social model of the *ayllu*"[41] (or, that is to say, the *ayllu* as a system—linking all social, economic, cultural, and political elements, an integral way of life, not divided or disassociated) is diffused through capillaries of the Andean social fabric until it permeates all the intersections of popular sociability. This long-term process of renewal (whose starting point could perhaps have been in the early twentieth century with the struggle against the all-powerful landlords), encompasses all facets of Andean social life: education, health, religion, land allocation, configuration of power, perception of time, and so on. The impression is that the logic of the *ayllu*—not whatever *ayllu*, but those that the Indians have reshaped throughout the twentieth century—is breaking into all areas of Aymara society and remodeling it from within, not by conquest but by an unplanned and natural outpouring that is both spontaneous and conscious. Note how in this long process of change, one that in reality configures a real revolution, the role of the state and the political parties—as articulators or protagonists—has been minimal, if nonexistent.

Toward a Multicultural State?

The cycle of protests and uprisings that began in 2000 with the Cochabamba water war and the Aymara insurgency in the Altiplano ended in a paradox: that the non-capitalist social relations and non-state powers that bolstered the movement would enthrone forces that seek to legitimize the state and expand capitalism. It would not be the first time that this has happened. The major revolutions in history (French, Russian, and Chinese) were all the product of the crisis of the state, and all resulted in a powerful reinforcement of the nation-state. In some form, the revolutions were a way of resolving the crisis of the state. "From the three revolutions, states emerged that were more centralized, more bureaucratic, and more powerful,

---

40 Interview with Silvia Rivera Cusicanqui.

41 Martín Castillo Collado, *Aprendiendo con el corazón. El tejido andino en la educación quechua* (La Paz: Pinseib, Proieb, Plural, 2005), 103.

both internally and externally."[42] Moreover, looking at the revolutions from below, one can conclude that workers and peasants "were more directly incorporated into national politics and the projects supported by the state in the wake of the revolutions, whose triumph they had helped ensure."[43]

One of the most distinguished Bolivian intellectuals and politicians, Alvaro García Linera (vice president of the government headed by Evo Morales) claims that the Bolivian state must "give way to a multicultural state, to include the sectors marginalized up to now—the indigenous, respecting their forms of community organization," with the objective of establishing "equality of political and cultural rights for all races and cultures in the country."[44] It is not the first time, as we shall see, that the Indian movement of the continent places the question of the multinational state at the center of their strategy.

The core of García Linera's contention is that in Bolivia there are four major systems of civilization: the modern industrial civilization, the domestic (informal) economy, the communal, and the Amazon civilization. But the state only represents the modern industrial civilization. The state has not been able to articulate the various social forces and organizational forms that coexist in Bolivia, so the goal then is to de-monopolize the presence of industrial civilization. He recognizes that there are non-liberal democratic practices that are not taken into consideration by the state and argues that "a substantive political leveling between cultures and identities requires a leveling in methods of producing policy at all levels of government."

But diversifying the state is not enough to equalize the differences in the legal field; it also requires leveling the various practices within the state apparatus. He proposes to "think of a punctual synchronicity, for short periods" between the various political practices in which "the traditional systems exist alongside the 'modern.'" Constitutional recognition for other political systems would be arrived at, alongside the formation of authorities and even the rotation of authorities in what would be a multi-civilization state:

> If Bolivia is a superimposing of various cultures and civilizations, the state should, as a synthesis, be an institution capable of articulating, of constituting a political

---

42   Theda Skocpol, *Los Estados y las revoluciones sociales* (México: FCE, 1984), 441.

43   Ibid., 440. In this sense the revolutions behave according to the concept coined by astronomy, as a star that completes an orbit in the sense of favoring the return of what had been removed, or weakened, in this case: the state.

44   Alvaro García Linera, "Democracia liberal vs. democracia comunitaria" in *El Juguete Rabioso* (La Paz, 20 January, 2004).

engineering formed by a proportional presence of the cultures and linguistic identities, as well as deliberative, representative, and assembly-based modern and traditional institutions making decisions on a general, "national" scale.[45]

The proposal, while maintaining a degree of abstraction, proposes "to constitute" and make the modern and traditional institutions compatible. Within the bosom of the state apparatus both the liberal and the community forms of decision making would coexist. In some cases the rotation of authorities would be used, supposedly providing a place for different democratic practices in the state.

For García Linera, the creation of a multinational and multi-civilization state in Bolivia (integrating ethno-cultural diversity into the institutional framework and in the distribution of powers) will establish "an enduring state order in the country."[46] The ultimate objective, explicitly stated, consists in overcoming cultural and social exclusion in order "to reconcile the state and society." This appears to be the fundamental tension that underlies this approach because, in line with Kymlicka, García Linera maintains that "the recognition of self-government for the national minorities contributes to the stability and cohesion of states."[47]

The new state would be born from the dual and simultaneous process of de-monopolizing the ethnicity of the colonial state and allowing "the other dominated and excluded ethnicities to share in social structures and political power."[48] García Linera defends a pact (proposed as "a pact-ist conception of power") to ensure "the articulation of plurality in the common political unit of a differential society," starting with regional autonomy, since self-government is what would allow each culture "to structure a system of political institutions that can reward, positively sanction collective cultural practices (language, dress, habits), and create a field of administrative, economic, and cultural competence based on a linguistic homogeneity."[49] In sum, the crucial point of the proposed multinational state is related to the need to "complete" that which until now indigenous societies do not have:

> What does not exist is a structure of self-government
> at a higher level among various communities, or among
> the hundreds or thousands of communities or urban

---

45 Ibid.
46 Alvaro García Linera, *Estado multinacional* (La Paz: Malatesta, 2005), 56.
47 Ibid., 64.
48 Ibid., 71.
49 Ibid., 72.

neighborhoods that are members of a large linguistic and cultural community—so that when members of these cultural communities are linked to the separate governmental administrations (economic, educational, administrative, police, or military), it must be done by abandoning their cultural knowledge (linguistic, oral, etc.), and the forced use of language, knowledge, and habits ambiguously learned from the dominant cultural identity that governs the state.[50]

Thus he defends the formation of autonomous, regional governments and autonomous regions—including, specifically, the possibility that the Aymara nationality constructs its own autonomous government and its own parliament "with full political competence" in a wide range of issues ranging from education, public administration, and taxes to policing and environmental resources.[51] He emphasizes that indigenous self-government "does not create centrifugal processes that lend themselves to separatist tendencies from the Bolivian state," which will remain "the superior political community." State reform is aimed at democratizing the political unit while preserving political and cultural diversity "through the constitutional integration of regional politico-indigenous communities into a superior political community," in which power is "shared and divided between a general government with national responsibilities and some constituent governments with responsibilities pertaining to the regional or sub-national."[52]

Finally, he believes that the key to ending ethnic exclusion—the objective for establishing the multinational state—is the equalizing of languages and cultural practices in public administration.[53] This would, for example, mean that ministerial positions at all levels would be mostly occupied by indigenous, as well as the integration of parliaments, regional governments, and the national government.

Elsewhere García Linera presents this proposal as complementary to the defense of what he terms as "Andino-Amazonian capitalism," which consists of the "non-brutal" (i.e. without violence) interpenetration of the modern, industrial economy and the Andean and Amazonian one.[54] He argues that the communal economy has clear limits for the development of Bolivia, without also noting the

---

50   Ibid., 73.
51   Ibid., 80.
52   Ibid., 85–86.
53   Ibid., 98.
54   Interview with Miguel Lora Fuentes to Alvaro García Linera, at www.bolpress.com

limits (ecological and social) of what he calls the modern or industrial economy. A central premise of his argument is his particular vision of the relationship between the modern and the traditional, which runs through the proposed construction of a multinational state, as seen in chapter four.[55] This quasi-Marxist modernizing vision (as if the famous controversy between Marx and Vera Zasúlich had never occurred[56]), seems to ignore the experience of the MNR since 1952 and especially the results obtained: the failure of the MNR to modernize or discipline the movement,[57] and from this the Katarist current emerged, among others, which is at the base of the Aymara movement. In the same vein, García Linera argues that for proper functioning of representative democracy, "the existence of non-capitalist productive structures, of non-commercial sharing schemes, are an obstacle to the constitution of equal subjects with the ability to take the market as the rational foundation of their social behavior, including the political."[58] Marx suggested that the Russian rural commune could be a platform for the construction of the new world of communism, but for García Linera, this "traditional" world is a barrier to change.

In his response to Zasúlich,[59] Marx points out that, at base, the capitalist system is the separation between producers and the means of production, which involves the expropriation of the peasantry. In *Capital*, he notes that the reasons for and against on the vitality of the Russian commune cannot be deducted, but a detailed study "has convinced me that this commune is the foundation of social regeneration in Russia."[60] Clearly Marx believed that non-capitalist relations can be beneficial—even in the construction of the new world—and moved away from any claims that capitalism (or the state or rep-

---

55   Alvaro García Linera, intervention in the Confrerencia Internacional "*Pensamiento y Movimientos sociales en América Latina.*" (Niteroi: Universidad Federal Fluminense-MST, 16 October, 2005).

56   Karl Marx and Federico Engels, *El porvenir de la comuna rural rusa* (México: Cuadernos de Pasado y Presente), 1980.

57   Translator's note: the Revolutionary Nationalist Movement (MNR) led the Bolivian National Revolution of 1952 and went on to hold political office for many of the ensuing years. The MNR, however, failed to live up to the expectations of the people and their policies were largely corporatist and assimilationist.

58   Alvaro García Linera, *Estado multinacional*, 51.

59   The populist Russian Vera Zasúlich had consulted Marx in 1881, on his opinion on whether the Russian rural commune should disappear under the capitalist development—as many of the social-democrats claimed—or could they "be developed along the socialist road." Karl Marx and Federico Engels, *El porvenir de la comuna rural rusa*, 29–30.

60   Ibid., 61.

resentative democracy) represents a step forward in the history of mankind.

Beyond these considerations, I wish to frame the proposed establishment of a multinational state in Bolivia in light of the experience of the Zapatista movement in Chiapas and the indigenous movement in Ecuador. The first emphasizes Indian autonomy, and the second the construction of a new state. For more than twenty years, both movements have been seeking to alter the relationship of forces and the distribution of powers between the national state, the people, and indigenous nations.

1) We are dealing with a proposal *born outside of the social movement*, unlike in Ecuador where the indigenous movement grouped themselves in the CONAIE (Confederation of Indigenous Nationalities of Ecuador) and devised the creation of a pluri-national state as a strategic objective. In Bolivia, no organization recognized by the social movement raised that flag, perhaps because events have taken a different path, consisting in the construction of Indian self-government. By contrast, in Bolivia the proposal arises from intellectuals associated with MAS.

As we have seen, the concept of state is not part of the Indian imagination. In times of serious confrontation with the Bolivian state, they created barracks such as Qalachaka, which are non-state centers of power under strict community control. The main evidence that García Linera enlists to defend his thesis that the Aymara are struggling for a state is an interview with Eugenio Rojas (mayor of Achacachi) during the 2003 blockades. Even here, the Aymara leader's statements clearly indicate that they do not want a state that is like the present one. "To recuperate our state, to recover our territory, and above all, our power, our state, and construct a new state which would be the Qullasuyu state. But with new characteristics, in terms of private property, or the form of doing politics, democracy as they call it."[61] Clearly, when Rojas uses the term "state," he is clearly referring to something quite different.

Lines below, the mayor of Achacachi makes it very clear that he is speaking of founding "a communitarian society," which would destroy the Bolivian state in order "to construct a new structure, under the system of our ancestors." Defining his terms, he said:

> There won't be an Executive Power, Legislative Power, or Judicial Power, that whole system. We are thinking of another kind of state ... because the moral question, reciprocity, *Ayni* (mutual aid), all these concepts do not

---

61   Alvaro García Linera, *Sociología de los movimientos sociales en Bolivia*, ibid., 194.

exist in the Bolivian state. All these issues break on the
notion of private property, the accumulation of capital
... it is not like that in the Qullasuyu because there are
other forces at play, those of reciprocity, of redistribution, working in mutual aid—in the sense, for example,
of communal property.[62]

In the proposed multinational state, community practices such
as *ayni*, the rotation of tasks, and others are recognized, but not in a
community context; they are instead placed in a state structure. How
could mutual aid be institutionalized in the state apparatus, separated from the community? It seems clear that certain practices cannot be separated from their context without distorting them greatly.
García Linera attempts to recognize mechanisms (which he terms
the "modes of producing politics" in Indian communities) and integrate them into the logic of the state. But in the process, they become
uprooted from the territory in which they are born. Can one conceive
of the functioning of "the traditional institutionalized systems" without the territorial base that sustains them and gives them meaning?
García Linera claims that these systems could be articulated within
the "modern," but would not such a proposal promote the subordination of the traditional to the modern, which has been around a long
time and forms part of the general common sense?

The rotation of authorities, to take another example, is a way
to prevent the formation of a separate, bureaucratic body, beyond
the control of the community. So, how is a practice of dispersing
bureaucracy and the state grafted into the bosom of the bureaucracy
and the state apparatus? On the other hand, doing tasks by shifts
and rotation has multiple applications, from regulating the use of water to participation in the blockades, in the same way that a system
of redistribution functions within the community. There is, as Patzi
points out, a communal system that has multiple dimensions and that
takes several forms. But what cannot be done is to take one of those
aspects, separate it, and transplant it to another context, because survival would be impossible, except as a "multinational" decoration in
the colonial state.

That is precisely what Eugenio Rojas says. Note the clear difference between the two: the Bolivian state with its three powers;
private property; and accumulation of capital; and that other "state"
the Qullasuyu, based on communal ownership, redistribution, reciprocity, and mutual aid. At this point, it must be said that using the
term "state" to refer to what would be the articulation based on the
communal system is much like what Mamani defined as a "semantic

---

62   Ibid., 195.

loan." It is inconceivable that a system created to prevent the concentration of power is crowned by a state, a state that is power concentrated and separated from society. In a beautiful and transparent text, García Linera himself confirms that the logic of the state is not part of the Aymara horizon:

> They organize the Qalachaka barracks: 40,000 Indians meet on this hillside, occupy it. The Bolivian army is here and the Aymara on the other side. "If they want to confront us, we will face them," they say, "and then we will go to La Paz and we will take the government." It is quickly said: "the state project of the insurgents" has appeared; they are planning to take the state. Their ambition is to take the state.
>
> But is their project a statist one? Their military organization was the most anti-statist ever seen in the world. Even more so than the Zapatistas. Because they were a sort of confederation of communities that decided today to cultivate the fields and tomorrow to go to war. And they came with their men, women, children, grandparents, and pets. They came as community going to war. Not as a formed group, not as an elite formed in the community. In the Qalachaka barracks, seventy-year-old women were armed with sticks, eighteen-year-old youths with FAL rifles, old men with dynamite, and children bringing the food. That is how it was in the Qalachaka barracks. And that has nothing to do with the state. There was no centralized control from above, there was no general staff. Command was something to be negotiated each day, according to the different community blocks that came. There was no leader, no commander. This is a very anti-statist logic.[63]

That is his description. However, when interpreting a few lines further down in the same text, García Linera says that the Qalachaka barracks "was a non-state with ambitions to be a real state." The truth is that the social movement has not proposed the creation of a multinational state, and everything related to the state—as pointed out by the vice president himself—is ambiguous. And confused. However, the indeterminacy within the Aymara movement toward the state does not allow for the conclusion that they were, in reality, looking for a way to create some kind of state. To claim as much

---

63 Colectivo Situaciones, *Mal de altura* (Buenos Aires: Tinta Limón, 2005, module 25).

would be to ignore both short-term and long-term history, in which the state is a figure outside of the Indian cosmovision.

2) The exercise of indigenous autonomy *precedes and creates the conditions for the construction of a larger unit,* be it a multi-ethnic or multinational state, because the new body cannot be continuous with the actual state but *something new or, that is, different, built from below.* As pointed out by Hector Díaz-Polanco, the hard nucleus of the political agenda of the Latin American indigenous movement is the demand for autonomy, so that the possibilities for "building a multi-ethnic and democratic state [depend] on the establishment of regimes of autonomy in the relevant national frameworks."[64]

This point is particularly obscured in the García Linera text (which does not mean that future developments will not further deepen this notion). Autonomy cannot be the result of a single act, but comes of a long process of construction, or better said, a process of social struggles; moreover, "it cannot be the product of a unilateral decision or an imposition, particularly by the government."[65] Likewise, there should not be a model of autonomy except that with a redistribution of capabilities and powers that are the nucleus of autonomy, that can be embodied in different forms depending on the conditions and needs of each people.[66] In García Linera's proposal, the question of autonomy appears too "closed," already defined and delineated, when it should be thought of as something open to experimentation. The objective, however, is to break with state centralism, based on the exercise of autonomy on several levels: communal, municipal, and regional.

Autonomy seeks to resolve the question of power, which is the cause of exclusion and marginalization of indigenous peoples. Said in another way, the exercise of political power will allow the people to exercise their rights, to determine their own priorities and control their own development, as specified by Convention 169 of the International Labor Organization (ILO), which establishes collective rights. However—as experience has shown the Zapatistas in Chiapas—communal, municipal, and regional autonomy seeks not only to

---

64   Héctor Díaz-Polanco, *La rebelión zapatista y la autonomía* (México: Siglo XXI, 1997), 15.

65   Ibid., 57.

66   For the EZLN and the Foro Nacional Indígena, "autonomy is a distribution of powers between different spheres of government, ranging from the communal, municipal, and regional levels, and should be conceived as a diversity of models and levels according to the needs of each people—integrating the right to territoriality, self-government, the full exercise of our legal systems; economic, social, and cultural development; and control of our internal security." In Héctor Díaz-Polanco, *Autonomía regional* (México: Siglo XXI, 1996), 239 onward.

change power relations from without, but also seeks to change things within the Indian peoples. Thus, Zapatista women do not separate the issue of autonomy from the issue of gender, because they conceive autonomy as a new integral relation, touching upon all aspects of life, both external and internal. Cultural and socio-economic inequalities, which had not previously been questioned or were seen as inevitable, "began to be perceived by the indigenous activists as a result of discrimination, exclusion, and their status as a *political minority*."[67]

In short, autonomy is part of the process of emancipation, through which one challenges one's inherited place in society, not just the institutional architecture. This is why it is inadequate to attempt to end exclusion, as García Linera proposes, by equalizing languages and cultural practices. While this is of great importance, it fails to highlight the role of political power—autonomy—as the real key to overcoming exclusion.

In both the Zapatista and Ecuadorian cases, they are trying to go beyond the actual state, to go even beyond capitalism. When the Ecuadorian indigenous organization created the CONAIE Political Project in 1994, the notion of a pluri-national state had a distinct anti-capitalist profile: it is the formula with which they reject and go beyond the "uni-national, bourgeois, white-mestizo state."[68] Moreover, it establishes a clear distinction between the old state and the pluri-national state, which it defines as "the political and legal organization of the peoples and nationalities of the country" that arises "when several peoples and nationalities come together under one government and constitution."[69]

The Zapatistas, meanwhile, have focused on the construction of autonomy, without defining what a new (multi)national state would be like. They have chosen to build autonomy from below, against the state, but have been careful to not outline the forms that it should take. This is not an omission, but an emphasis: whatever it is that they build, the commitment is in building actual autonomies that will, eventually, be linked with other autonomous regions to make way for a new consensus among all the constituents. The end is not the national state but autonomy, that is to say indigenous self-government.

3) The state *cannot contain plurality and multiplicity*. In their assessment of CONAIE's proposed pluri-national state, Ecuadorian analysts saw a serious contradiction. They questioned the term "state"

---

67   Héctor Díaz-Polanco, *México diverso* (México: Siglo XXI, 2002), 115.

68   Confederación de Nacionalidades Indígenas de Ecuador (CONAIE), *Proyecto Político*, 2001, www.conaie.org.

69   Ibid.

because it would be inconsistent with the concept of "multicultural" given that it constrains the creation of an alternative society: "I think the notion of 'state,' as a centralized power, traps and puts limits on the utopianism of the construction of a society that is pluri-cultural, just, compassionate, and based on the best traditions of the diverse cultures of Ecuador."[70]

Even in a country like Ecuador, where the state presence is very different from that of Bolivia, where the racist and colonial state became resigned early on to integrating the Indians (the revolution of 1952 resolved to integrate them, but as peasants), the institutional state is unable to contain the diversity and difference:

> The Indian alternative must be to create a pluricultural way of thinking; that is, a set of bridges that unite the various forms of Indian resistance with various modes of non-Indian resistance; Indian initiatives and proposals with the utopian ideas of the ecologists, the suppression of gender differences, suppression of the classes, and the humanism of the Christian communities.... Surely, the result will be beyond the imagination or the state, pointing to forms of self-organization of society, *without the shackles of centralized power*: it is for this reason that the Indian struggle will not be centrally directed to improve the state, although that is a necessary task, but to strengthen the society against the state.[71]

The project of the Indians goes beyond a state that does not stop being a national state. They perceive power in another form, based on a self-organized pluricultural society starting out from the Andean community paradigm, which includes a harmonious relationship with nature, holistic systems of thought and a different relationship with time and space, no longer split but integrated. In sum, it is a civilized project that is different from Western capitalism and does not revolve around state power.[72]

It is worth dwelling a little on the process in Ecuador, because in a period of twenty years the Indians went to build an organization that contains all nationalities that gave birth to the strategic project of a multicultural state. They led several uprisings and, after the 2003 election victory of Lucio Gutiérrez, formed part of the government. In this long process, they succeeded in convening a Constituent Assembly that gained recognition for the collective rights of Indians

---

70   Galo Ramón Valarezo, *El regreso de los runas* (Quito: Comunidec, 1993), 239–240.

71   Ibid., 240. My emphasis.

72   Ibid., 276–277.

and for Ecuador as a plurinational state. The evaluation of this process is that, having assumed a logic of power, the Indian movement went into crisis and is now unraveling.

In January 2005, the *Ary Rimay Bulletin* of the Scientific Institute of Indigenous Cultures (ICCI in its Spanish acronym), headed by the Quechua leader Luis Macas, published a long article assessing the recent history of the movement (this was immediately after the CONAIE concluded a conference at which it chose Macas as president and began its reconstruction after its disastrous involvement in Lucio Gutiérrez's government). It argues that building alliances with other social movements, the project of a pluri-national state, the construction of an inter-cultural society, participation in state institutions, a decade of mobilizations, electoral intervention, and brief involvement with the Gutiérrez government—in addition to showing the power of the movement—"was weakening and limiting the real scope of their political project."[73]

The text grounds its analysis in paradoxes: progress reveals weaknesses, gains become prisons. But an unresolved problem lies in the background: the question of power and the state. It notes that the Ecuadorian political system is "a 'locus' that condenses, structures, and normalizes relations of power in society, and that adopts strategies and measures to confront and limit the possibilities of the indigenous movement as a political and historical subject," to the point where "it becomes one of the strongest barriers created by the power structure for the sake of destroying the indigenous movement as a political interlocutor." Thus, the gains (such as adoption of collective rights by the Constituent Assembly) become the beginning of a political defeat for the Indian project, by closing off democratic spaces under the control maintained by the elite of the political system.

To run for elections, CONAIE founded the Pachakutik Movement in 1995. In addition to problems arising from being first a social movement and second a political one, the article comes to a conclusion that is non-ideological though the result of a decade's experience: "To change the state from within its own institutions is virtually impossible." And it adds: "The political system, and similarly the economic system, cannot be changed with legal reforms, but only with mobilizations, resistance, and the struggle against power." That is, by the social movement. The editorial insists that these points were clear to CONAIE throughout the 1990s, but that the creation of Pachakutik changed relations between "the social" and "the political," rendering the latter autonomous from the former or, to put it differently, separating the electoral apparatus and the leaders from the "social"

---

73 "Los dilemas de la CONAIE," *Boletín Ary Rimay* (Quito: ICCI, No. 70, January 2005).

part. When the movement progressed enough to create a crisis for the institutional state, a similar thing happened in both Ecuador and Bolivia: "The temptations of power were too strong to resist, without believing the fallacy of being government and having power." The result of participation in government was dramatic. In less than six months, the movement realized that "its historical project was valid only if it took a radical stance and directly confronted the political system as a whole, which is to say, the system of domination and power." The result, as everyone knows, is that the movement emerged from the experience of government with its legitimacy weakened and eroded, although the state was unable to fracture it.

On the other hand, during the critical political scenario of 2000, CONAIE made a radical shift, according to Pablo Dávalos, an economist and adviser to the organization. The movement in the 1980s and 1990s moved from the struggle for land to the struggle for a pluri-national state, and in the conjuncture of January 2000 "a rupture was made with the previous demands, while at the same time opening a new dimension in organizational dynamics: that of power."[74] For the Indian movement, which had been constructed as a counter-power, erecting itself as an alternative power meant "a series of ruptures involving the risk of a serious fracture of the organizational cohesion and the mobilization of the social movement." One cannot be power (the state) and counter-power (anti-state mobilization) at the same time:

> It assumes the logic of power can lead to the destruction of the experience gained as a counter-power. That is to say, this accumulated history of strikes, national work stoppages, indigenous revolts, and uprisings could prove counterproductive to governing, managing, and negotiating institutional spaces and political society.... To become a power, the social movement would have needed to control, disperse, or destroy the forms of resistance and forms of counter-power they had generated against the government.[75]

The state is unable to contain plurality and multiplicity, unless it integrates them as a homogenized unit. Similarly, counter-powers cannot be converted into power without annulling their multiple potencies. Centralized state power forces the movement to delegate to a handful of representatives and professionals the defense of their interests in the state. By doing so, it disarms the movement, under-

---

74 Pablo Dávalos, "Ecuador: las transformaciones políticas del movimiento indígena ecuatoriano" (Buenos Aires: *OSAL* No. 1, Clacso, June 2000), 25.

75 Ibid., 29.

mining its strength; the intensity of the experience is neutralized by representation.

Institutions codify social relations, and to counteract this process, all that is left is individual and collective flight, a multiple desertion — the intensity of an action that cannot be represented.

4) Pursuing the objective of a multicultural state, and therefore accepting a logic of state power, goes hand in hand with the *unification and centralization of the social movement, thus annulling its capacity for dispersal*. After centralization comes co-optation. Once again, the example of Ecuador is a mirror into which we gaze. In this case, "the reference to state power is one that serves as a pivotal political moment," encouraging the separation and lack of accountability of a set of leaders.[76]

CONAIE introduced the pluri-national state proposal as an attempt to modify its internal structure, which was then interpreted as "an attempt to centralize ... the colorful and diverse organizational process in each province and each region into a single organization."[77] It was an internal process of homogenization, fortunately incomplete, in which the reconstitution of the nationalities from which to negotiate with the state meant the forced resolution of inter-communal conflicts, within the grassroots organizations and federations, and then in the national organizations, in order to find a common space for designating authorities of the nationalities and peoples. The process, which resulted in "a sort of para-statal space of confluence and organization,"[78] culminated in the First Congress of the Peoples and Nationalities in October 2001.

At the moment when organizational unity was created in spite of internal differences, the foundation was laid for participation in the government of Lucio Gutiérrez, a move consolidated a year later. In the same process that set in motion the unity of the 2001 congress, the Pachakutik political movement underwent "a strong tendency to make independent and centralize the functioning apparatus," against those who advocated for "the old tradition of decentralized Indian organizations."[79]

As part of that same process, the Indian leaders were co-opted — or at least enough of them to weaken the movement as a whole. The Indigenous and Black Peoples of Ecuador Development Project (PRODEPINE in its Spanish acronym), financed by the World

---

76 Fernando Guerrero and Pablo Ospina, *El poder la comunidad*, ob. cit. p. 230.

77 Ibid., 189.

78 Ibid.

79 Ibid., 232.

Bank in the 1990s, prioritized strategies that tried to guide the move-ment toward an exclusively ethnic discourse, reducing it to ethnic demands. This can be summarized as "managing works and pro-grams in exchange for avoiding uprisings."[80]
Likewise, the movement's participation in development initia-tives, and the changes that the system itself promoted in rural areas, produced multiple diversification of indigenous societies: differences arising from structural economic conditions were added to the al-ready existing local historical differences. But overall, these outside interventions promoted the diversification of the social configuration of the Indian leaders, a carefully planned process overseen by world development agencies:

> A sensitive transfer of leaders who came from a peasant background to the position of functionaries and medium and higher level professionals... Teachers, state officials, and technical workers from development projects stood out. They have also diversified organizational and politi-cal expressions of the indigenous world: from a source strongly rooted in the open assemblies, they have es-pecially proliferated associations, youth, and women's groups, second-degree organizations, federations, and the structures of political representation. Finally, there has been a diversification of institutions and external actors involved in the indigenous world: if for the most part the Church and political activists from the left pre-viously filled the space abandoned by the large estates and political lieutenants, now there is a proliferation of development projects from the state and private organi-zations.[81]

In sum, the achievements of the mobilization created a new scenario, which is basically used by the powers to weaken and de-stroy the movement. Among these particularly dangerous new sce-narios are the spaces of political representation and the bonds that they generate. The question of power and the state, which seems to have entered the movement as a "natural" consequence of its growth, is nevertheless a profound burden introduced from outside. For global elites who want to destroy the Indian movements, the strategy of development and that of power or participation in the state (that are two sides of the same coin) can be interpreted as a sort of "low intensity warfare" against Indians.

---

80   Ibid., 255.
81   Ibid.

In the case of Ecuador, the two analyses cited converge on one point: on one side, the "permeability" of the state to ethnic demands "encourages the organizational direction with concrete achievements and encourages the multiplication of indigenous leaders" who are co-opted by the same process that creates or attempts to create them."[82] In parallel, the pro-development strategies are a "Trojan horse whose purpose is to destroy the political project of the indigenous movement," because they undermine the foundations of the movement and the communities, and are conduits to electoral participation, being embedded in the state and assuming the logic of representation. Both complementary logics have undermined the movement that, ultimately, came to understand that being in government meant "its historical project was valid only if it took a radical and direct confrontation with the political system as a whole, that is to say, *against the system of domination and power*."[83] It would be a pity if other movements did not learn from the Ecuadorian experience.

5) Participation in the state—even if it is to build a multinational state, starting necessarily from the colonial state—*gives rise to a faction of Indian officials separated from their communities* who form a new functional elite for the system of domination. At this point the policy of the multinational state and development converge, because both can only be realized through the creation of this Indian elite, who become, in fact, a means of subordinating the movement to outside interests, in what constitutes a strategy of "envelopment and assimilation." Hector Díaz-Polanco has defined this as *etnofagia*, literally, ethnic-devouring.[84]

In Latin America, the indigenous struggle to overcome exclusion has been answered by the various states not with ethnocide, as in previous periods, but in new ways that operate as "socio-cultural magnets deployed by the national state and the apparatus of hegemony to attract, displace, and dissolve the different groups."[85] With this objective, the states "assume" respect for difference, going as far as "protecting" Indian cultures by getting the Indians themselves (through their leaders and intellectuals) to become advocates of integration. But for this policy of assimilation to get results—or, that is, for the destruction of Indian cultures to be overseen without ethnocide—a group of leaders separated from their communities must be created to become the vehicle for integration.

---

82   Ibid., 256.
83   "*Los dilemas de la CONAIE*," *Boletín Ary Rimay*. My emphasis.
84   Hector Díaz-Polanco *Autonomía regional*, 99.
85   Ibid., 97.

Here the politics of a multinational state, and the politics of development and ethnicity driven by international agencies through NGOs, have a shared outlook. It is not that García Linera is the sponsor of this current, but that his proposal arises in the midst of a process so that it, beyond the author's will, tends to be part of that same current. Note what happened in Ecuador in the 1980s.

A thorough investigation in the indigenous province of Chimborazo reveals "the links between the proliferation of NGOs and the degree of organizational density of the indigenous/peasant world."[86] The research notes the close relationship between the volume of indigenous population, and the NGOs operating there, and concludes that it is the massive presence of NGOs that explains the proliferation of second-degree organizations. It highlights "the desire expressed by NGOs and financiers to consolidate interlocutors," representing the beneficiaries and as spokespeople to ensure that interventions have the greatest possible repercussions.[87] The second-degree organizations (federations, associations) arise with close links to development programs and are, therefore, driven by external motives. It is here, within these organizations formed to manage the resources of international cooperation, that "the formation of leadership elites takes place." These elites become increasingly distanced from their bases and compete among themselves to become beneficiaries of the NGOs, thereby generating conflicts between organizations.

For the indigenous movement, the problem is twofold: elites arise where before there had been none, and these have very different characteristics from the previously existing forms of movement leadership. If the former leaders had a militant and ideological character, with a politico-militant profile, the new leadership elite would have a technocratic character because they are now better able to interact with external agents—those who "end up consolidating a complex network of favors rendered in exchange for future support."[88] These elites, enthroned by their ability to attract external resources, have been defined by the anthropologist Victor Breton as "the new-style chieftains." He coincides with Díaz-Polanco in defining these policies as *etnofagias*, since they seek the domestication of the indigenous movement by placing ethnicity at a "politically correct" level in accord with the demands of globalization: "The ascension of pluri-culturalism, pluri-lingualism, and in the best case, pluri-nationality

---

86   Víctor Bretón Solo de Zaldívar, "Capital social, etnicidad y desarrollo: algunas consideraciones críticas desde los Andes ecuatorianos" (Quito: *Yachaikuna* No. 2, ICCI, December 2001), 10.

87   Ibid., 11.

88   Ibid., 12.

of the Latin American states need not be antagonistic to the logic of neoliberal capitalist accumulation."[89]

In effect, international cooperation proposed to strengthen the indigenous movement's organizations, with the result that a good part of the indigenous intelligentsia responsible for setting up the movement in the 1980s now "live and work entrenched in the bureaucratic and administrative machinery of development."[90] In the canton of Guamote, province of Chimborazo, where thirty development agencies are working, there now exist twelve second-degree and 158 first-degree organizations for 28,000 rural inhabitants; yet it remains one of the poorest cantons in the country with the highest percentage of homelessness. The final conclusion is devastating:

> The experience of the Ecuadorian Andes shows their [the NGOs'] tremendous limitations as entities to alleviate poverty, and their exceptional efficiency in co-opting and encapsulating the intermediate levels of the indigenous movement.... The main priority is whatever one tells oneself [it is] and is justified by any means possible—they are no longer productive projects *in the strict sense*, but a framework for corralling local elites and prominent Indian intellectuals into the pro-development machinery.[91]

Something similar is happening in Bolivia, since the agencies that plan policies are the same throughout the world: the World Bank, and, in the case of Bolivia, USAID. As happened across the Andes, following the defeat of the rebellions of Tupac Amaru and Tupac Katari and the beheading of the Aymara and Quechua aristocracy, the Indians lost the ability to express and represent themselves. A new possibility for recuperation emerged in the second half of the twentieth century when the Indians converted themselves into subjects once more through the struggle for education, the birth of a new generation of indigenous intellectuals, and the articulation of a new Indian movement. The new policies are a response to Indian intervention, and everything indicates that steps taken in Ecuador will be followed in Bolivia, appropriate to the circumstances of this country.

To avoid misunderstandings, it should be clarified that the proposed multinational state could form part, if they do not take the necessary precautions, of an *etnofagia* policy designed by international cooperation agencies like the World Bank. In this sense, the Zap-

89 Ibid., 13.
90 Ibid.
91 Ibid., 16.

atista experience can be a reference point, since they have decided to build their own autonomy with their own resources, explicitly rejecting state "support" and international cooperation—but open to grassroots (and non-statist) global solidarity.

6) The Aymara Community subject (in the Aymara world, a social subject outside of the community framework does not exist) constitutes itself autonomously, which is what distinguishes it from other subjects. While the working class cannot be understood without the bourgeoisie, the peasants without landlords, women without patriarchy, the unemployed without work, *the Aymara movement has another genealogy: it does not necessarily refer to the oppressor, but to its own history and its short and long memories.* Both the Aymara history and long memory completely precede the colonial period—although colonialism does determine its mode of expression.

Since the Tiwanaku Manifesto, the main reference of the current Aymara movement is not the state or colonial society, but the distant past—the cosmovision and Andean religions and the community system, which together inspire the future and the objectives of the movement. It is not constructed as a mirror or a reflection, but it is what gives autonomy to the Aymara (and perhaps also the Quechua and Guarani, among others). It begins from an integrated logic—integrating the "cultural" and "political" into an inseparable totality, assuming the discourse as a people and nation and not just as a class. Variables are introduced that emphasize that statism does not occupy a prominent place.

We postulate that this characteristic is linked to the non-capitalist nature of the Andean communities, to the existence of another truly different world, with its other economy, its other politics, its other society and culture. For the communities, the political system with its parties, its state, and its police are still something foreign.

The state and capitalism are inseparable. The separation of the economic and the political, one of the premises of capitalism, is inherent in the system and part of the separation between producers and means of production; separation of what is construed as society and that which contributes to consolidating and perpetuating it.[92]

A society like the Aymara is one in which producers and the product are not separated, where production takes place without external control (boss or foreman), where there is no medicine because the community has the power to heal, nor schooling because access to knowledge does not require the intervention of any other person

---

92   John Holloway, *Cambiar el mundo sin tomar el poder* (Buenos Aires, Herramienta, 2002), 58–59.

except oneself.[93] It is a society in which capitalism has no way of latching on and prospering. A society founded in the *ayllu*, conceived as a system articulating all social, economic, cultural, and political elements, and as a way of living with intimacy and trust,[94] that does not know the subject-object relationship, and that presents no opportunity for capitalism and the state to prosper within its bosom.

Similarly, when that society is set in movement, when it mobilizes its non-capitalist social relations, it does not need to be mirrored or reflected in the other (boss, state) to be identified as its opposite, but garners inspiration from its own cosmovision; and in this way the mobilization integrates all aspects of that society: the flags and ceremonial horns, rituals and authorities, protest and party. There being no separation, when the society mobilizes, it does so in an integral manner, leaving nothing out. For this reason there is no space for political parties, which in the Aymara world they—although present— have always been a parasitic excrescence.

Aymara Ambiguities

One cannot but note a strong ambiguity within the Indian movement throughout this discussion and the debates around it—an ambiguity that "navigates between several options that intersect, separate, and fork: whether to oppose the power of the state, to become state power, or to create spaces more or less autonomous from the power within the state."[95]

Fundamentally, it is not about ideological options. The point is that everyday life of "Indian society," including of course the *ayllu*, is permeated by those options—which intersect at certain times, are separated at others and then bifurcate, not as a linear process of consecutive states but in a simultaneous manner. Although the *ayllu* affirms its autonomy in its daily life, self-organization and self-government, clientele relationships, and submission to the state or its leaders characterize that same everyday life, in order to cover the needs or expectations that the *ayllu* is unable or unwilling to lose sight of. For that reason, Indian reality cannot be understood as pure opposition to the state, but rather as a creation of autonomous spaces or powers within the state, including incumbent desires to become the state. This book, taking the Indian mobilizations as a starting point and epistemological hub, has emphasized the potencies that are

---

93   Martín Castillo Collado, *Aprendiendo con el corazón. El tejido andino en la educación quechua* (La Paz: Pinseb-Proieb-Plural, 2005), 102.

94   Ibid.,103.

95   Fernando Guerrero and Pablo Ospina, *El poder la comunidad*, 233.

deployed in those moments, knowing that they are just that: potencies, not accomplished realities.

As Colectivo Situaciones has expressed with great subtlety,
the ambiguity is related to the deployment of potencies and Aymara
mobilization: "The ambiguity is the way that a world of forces and
energies are presented without stabilities;" which take the form of "a
continuous swinging between dissolution and dispersion on the one
hand, and cohesion and the organic on the other."[96]

An unstable world. Forcibly unstable. Internally, because having no leader or state—and not being anchored in the subject-object
relationship—it is open to the flow, not as an option, but as something inherent in that world. In relation to the external world, the
colonial era and its continuation in the form of the Republic forces
them into a deep nomadic existence of motionless travel, consistently
de-constructing and dispersing against the outside oppressor in an
attempt not to become a carbon copy of the same.

This radical ambiguity of Indian society, linked to a multiplicity of factors—ranging from their own contradictory history to the
cultural mix and social inevitabilities—cannot, or should not, settle
in favor of only one of the options involved. Nevertheless, from an
ethical and emancipatory point of view, none of the options are com-
parable. Because emancipation is, in large measure, casting off the
oppressive aspects of our own traditions and practices, and empowering those that strengthen liberation and autonomy. Thus, the Indian ambiguity, which forms part of the radical ambiguity of human
beings—surviving between emancipation and subordination—will
not be solved by removing one of its extreme moments, but by riding
the waters of life at the helm leaning toward the side of emancipation, or be it toward the non-state, knowing that the very inertia of
life-navigation impels us—perhaps inevitably so—toward the reconstruction of institutions, the state, oppression.

---

96   Colectivo Situaciones, *Mal de Altura* (Buenos Aires: Tinta Limon, 2005).

Notes about the Notion of "Community"

Apropos of Dispersing power

Movements as Anti-state Forces

1. We just finished reading *Dispersing Power: Social Movements as Anti-State Forces*. The potency of the current "Bolivian moment" comes out clearly in the text. The hypothesis, summed up from the title itself, places us squarely in front of the current political challenge: it's about persevering within the point of view of the struggles and their underlying modes of resistance. This is the authentic key to, and the motor for, the long processes of disorganization of the centralized and diffused instances of colonial capitalist power that are today visible on a global scale.

As Raquel Gutiérrez Aguilar says in her prologue [to the Tinta Limón edition, 2006], there is a fundamental juncture in the Bolivian situation: either the political, organizational, and interpretive modes are found that deepen the democratic flow of the re-appropriation of the means of life and creation, or a phase of movement destabilization is inaugurated, restricting the potentialities of the process, in the name of a supposed gradualism.

In this context, the hypothesis of a "community in movement" as an irreplaceable and immediate element of the process leads us to directly consider not so much possible directions or foreseeable transformations, but rather the very way that we represent this vital flow, these persistent nuclei of resistance that are effective both in disorganizing power (dispersing it) as well as simultaneously producing renewed openings and social imaginations.

It is for this reason that the notion of community interests us. And not in a purely speculative way, but rather concretely, as it appears to us when we concern ourselves with the emancipatory dimension of the processes taking place.

These notes, then, are not a conclusion to Raúl Zibechi's book, but rather extend certain ongoing discussions regarding ways of conceiving notions of the common and the communitarian.

2. The notion of *community* rightly weighs heavily in each of the theorems deduced by *Dispersing Power*, and it presides over each of the argumentative strategies, from the moment in which the book tries to prevent community from becoming a general category—one useful for naming an infinite number of different objects—but rather a specific concept for an historical, social transformation: community is the name for an organizational and political code determined as a singular social technology. It combines a very particular aptitude: the arrival, through images of other times—and of another way of imagining time itself—of actualized collective energies. Community, in movement, itself movement, develops thusly as an alternative efficacy, where we perceive an unusual gratitude through relationships. In this way, community names an always alert, and always generous disposition toward the common. Without a doubt, this way of conceiving community-form is taken, here, to its positive limit. The text has taken to extremes its characteristics, its emancipatory potential, in order to develop urgent battles against its modernizing anachronization, but also in order to reveal, in contrast to other current approaches to life, the existence of sensible and political forces that put it in movement. Community operates, in this text, as a naming of the forms of collective action; and it does so with the intention of going against the grain of that evanescent sensibility for whom all that is sold melts into air.

3. Community, then, deserves new attention, not as an eccentricity of the past that resists dying, but as a dynamic of both common production and common association with overwhelming political relevance, although it is as plagued with ambivalence as it is vital. Thinking about community means conceiving its real dynamic: moving, clearly, but also detaining and metastasizing (just as Alex de la Iglesia's film *Comunidad* reminds us, as well as Bolivian voices, like Mario Galindo's "what happens if indigenous self-affirmation rots on us along the way?"). It must be a community perceived without either aprioriisms or folklore-isms (one that frustrates our comprehension of the ways in which *the communitarian* is reinvented), and above all that is not reduced to a plenitude that has been deproblematized and disconnected from other segments of social cooperation (which it ends up doing at its closures, its substantializations).

On the contrary, thinking about community in its dynamic and potential implies observing the processes of constant dissolution, in order to later understand the unprecedented ways in which it re-articulates itself in other spaces (from the country to the city), in other times (from the peripheral crisis of Fordism to the neoliberal crisis), in other images (from the *people* to the neighborhood council), in which *the common* holds other possibilities while it faces other conflicts. Community is not recognizable when thought of as a continuous thread in the history of certain Latin American regions or as a persistent subject in time, rather it tends toward a condition deciphered as a combination of traits that—often inopportunely— embody *the commune*.

4. *Community* is a particular, historical configuration of the *common*. The common as a virtuality that pulsates and is made manifest in the community, but doesn't live fulfilled within it. Community with its alienated and re-created zones, as a space of dispute and a horizon of communist vitality. Community as a collection of predetermined procedures, which arise and develop in a broken line of alterations, more like a gene and an impassible inheritance. Community, therefore, as the bearer of memory and a know-how, a reserve of images and a connector between the link and existence, and resembling a factory of discourses and slogans of current struggles, in contrast with its own inertias. Thus community is movement insofar as it is an effort to bring the common up to date, and the common is always that which is not absolutely realizable—it is an open universality, unable to be grasped in its totality. Community is always, and because of that, a coming about, an intent, a step forward. It is from there as well that its closures and detainments distance it from the common, or they minimize it, outlining a "community without the common."

Interrogating Bolivia by way of *the common* means trying to capture the laboratory of a *communitarian* social machine (emerged and developed in the formula: autonomy + cooperation) while in action. It is difficult not to see in that "function" a *production* (of the common under a·*communitarian* form) and a *proliferation* (of *the common* way beyond the formal limits of the communities themselves), more than a simple mobilization of resources and completely anterior logic, always pre-existent. It is also difficult not to assume this social invention in all its complexity: idealization of *the common* means becoming distracted from the permanent process of *the common* construction, a cop-out in terms of understanding the oppressive and hierarchal logics that enclose upon it (detainments and closings) and that permanently challenge its reformulations.

Community, then, develops as a space of particular and historical configuration of *the common* and *the common* as something virtual that beats like a heart and is actualized in the community, but does not live realized within it.

5. *Lo común* is played out in the relationship between the *communitarian* impulse and the colonial, racist, and capitalist sate. But this relationship is not destined to be a return of the anachronistic over a modern frustration. To the contrary, the *communitarian* task and its openness to internal contradiction and ambivalences inform us of the radical contemporaneousness of community with respect to other modes of cooperation and social organization. At the same time, the colonial-capitalist state, in addition to producing the worst internal hierarchies, has been a very concrete brake on the development of new subjective and political powers. The Bolivian social movements, then, are bearers of a new modernity, up until now submerged.

6. *The communitarian*, then, is a dynamic of economic and subjective production. More than a model for ensuring a cohesive unit without fissures, it activates by way of a permanent differentiation. Community tends to chemically reproduce its molecules (social cooperation and autonomy), evading concentration and attacking (dispersing) centralizing instances, molds, and methods imposed upon its development. Community, against all common sense, produces dispersion. A dispersion even more paradoxical in the measure that it constitutes the very possibility of its fluidity: it evades the crystallization of initiatives or the freezing up of groups into institutional or state forms and at the same time electrifies popular energies. Dispersion, as a way of returning to the common, insists on combating its alienation into fixed and closed forms, including the closing up of the collective into pure communities. The community that is best defined by its itinerant mutations (migrations, re-localizations, etc.) appears to give a place to this constant movement that makes of dispersion its common strength.

Dispersion, itself, as that opposed to accumulation and concentration, but also dispersion of that which fixes and shapes it. Dispersion of power, war on the state. Dispersion against centralization.

It would be an error, however, to identify this dispersive logic with isolation or with the absence of relations. Everything completely the contrary is the case: dispersion as a transversal connection, as an increase in cooperation. Community subjectivity emerges as a rupture of any disciplinarian rules about cooperation, about the base of the dispersion of power.

7. Autonomy, we propose, cannot be conceived as a restrictive self-sufficiency, save for the multiple conditions and influences, which would do nothing more than reproduce the liberal ideal of the rational subject, asserted in its economic, intellectual, and moral independence. On the contrary, autonomy as a political trait of cooperation, is unthinkable without delving into global interaction, connected with

many actors and powers of all stripes. If, in spite of that immersion, autonomy can be reclaimed by so many experiences as a political trait, it can also be said to be an orientation to concrete developments that begin from the powers themselves, and its fundamental decision to make its productions circular without the latter being expropriated by the mediating-expropriating instances of the state and capital. The "internal times" and the "capacity of subtraction" are relevant to any experience of autonomy, but they are also, if frozen, dogmas that entirely exhaust its perspective. It is from this point that autonomy does not oppose totalizing (as a movement of opening), rather it opposes a "given totalizing" (as a movement of closing and closure) — to the extent that, strictly speaking, no political situations arise. It is rather precisely at the beginning of an autonomous movement of the production of the common that they arise, be it that the movement leads to rupture and polarization, aiming to displace the limits of the situation, or be it pushing a shift characterized by cooperation over the displaced limit. There is no greater political anachronism than that of delaying these social temporalities.

8. It is fitting here to distinguish dispersion, produced by social movements, from fragmentation, which is promoted by the market and the state. Really there should not be confusion between one and the other: while dispersion, avoiding centralization, feeds the flow of cooperation; fragmentation molds it and subordinates it to the logic of capital. While dispersion connects, neoliberal fragmentation makes hierarchies and concentrates from above. Current ambivalence demands the distinction between both dynamics, without losing sight of the fact that dispersive tendency is itself woven throughout the dominant context of capitalist fragmentation. The confusion of language in favor of fragmentation comes not just from those who actively promote it (NGOs and international financial organizations) but also from those who subordinate the construction of transverse relations to unity from above (state) instead as the only form of struggle against fragmentation. Bolivia displays, in the current moment, the encounter between the *communitarian* dynamic — with its double movement of destructive dispersion and constructive cooperation — and the dynamic of the colonial-state in crisis. This open situation puts in play the depth of the democratizing impact of social movements upon the state, as well as institutional persistence and orientation toward metamorphosis.

9. Under neoliberalism, the processes of fragmentation, privatization, and exploitation of the commons expropriates resources and unravels *communitarian* webs at the same time that it pushes toward new struggles in which *the common* is recomposed. But this construc-

tive movement is realized in a new terrain, overwhelming the old framework of the nation-state community and multiplying the dimensions at play in terms of production of *the common*, until not only is the struggle against racism and colonialism involved, but there is also the re-appropriation of natural resources, public services, and the symbolic position of *the communitarian* in political life. In Bolivia urban indigenous reorganization, the struggle for the public management of water, and the nationalization of gas all unfold according to this logic. The challenge in thinking *the communitarian* cannot but come from this new composition of *the common* and its dynamics that contain the re-appropriation of natural resources and the self-regulation of the social relations that emerge in these struggles. The most recent traits of the emerging governability of the continent is the recognition of these tendencies (effective even if partial or mediated by representation) in which the most notable threat is precisely the attempt to control and stabilize the street strength of the movements. From this point of view, any attempt to reduce the current forms of *the common* either to state-nation-development-ist models or to an endogenous close over community—indigenous-traditional becomes ingenuous or directly reactionary.

10. Community against state, then, presumes that there is a contrast between productive flows and the oppressive management of those energies. Neoliberalism had already figured out this polar relationship, openly connecting communities with the capitalist market without mediations. El Alto and the new resistances emerge (and are constructed) in this open confrontational dynamic. The current crisis of the apparatus of domination in Bolivia implies a general reformulation between state and society, between state and community. Re-composition of a (new) state-ability based on the recognition of a dynamic of *communitarian* struggle? How to evaluate this apparently novel situation that has opened up in Bolivia? To what extent will this new polarity now develop? Will a new political composition of the state emerge from the full recognition of the *communitarian* dynamic and its dispersive powers or will there be a new attempt to subordinate it? Either way, one can easily see that the crossroads at which Bolivia currently finds itself are determined by the recognition of the dispersive power of the *communitarian*, but also by the need to develop greater forms of cooperation on a new scale, while at the same time combating their own tendencies to close themselves up and against the state-capitalist forces that promote this closing. The development of new powers that are based on a recognition of the *communitarian* dynamic (lead by obeying) appears to be the key to a new political constitution in Bolivia.

11. We arrive at a new formula: dispersion of power plus social cooperation. It appears that *communitarian* dispersion has learned to confront the mechanisms of subjective fragmentation and capitalist-state centralization, and now has a dual challenge of configuring means of collective regulation in accord with the logic of dispersion, anticipation, and destruction of state centralization. A positive productive force and a negative dispersive force. The first requires forms that are more widely able to articulate cooperation and the second, with Clastres, is conquered with "bosses who do not give orders."

12. All over the continent, with the movements' great differences in development, self-reference capability, and struggle (that is, not only the large social organizations but also the dynamics of collective action), the same question arises: what is to be done with the state? The question of who governs and how, in the context of movements destabilizing the scene in recent decades, is now urgent. How to conceive the solidification of the heterogeneous development of the capitalist states on behalf of the movements? Develop non-state powers? Should the movements try out a new advanced dynamic against the governments that govern in their name? Combine a double movement of struggle and coexistence by building counter-power non-state institutions against state institutions of power? At any rate, the dual perspective of dispersing power and inventing ample modes of cooperation seems to be the formula of the active principle being played out in the "Bolivian moment."

Bibliography

Albó, Xavier (1979) *Achacachi: medio siglo de lucha campesina*, Cipca, La Paz.

———. (2002) *Pueblos indios en la política*, Cipca, Cuaderno de Investigación No. 55, La Paz.

Albó, Xavier y Barrios, Raúl (1993) *Violencias encubiertas en Bolivia*, Cipca-Aruwiyiri, La Paz.

Albó, Xavier y Quispe, Víctor (2004) *Quiénes son indígenas en los gobiernos municipales*, Cipca-Plural, La Paz.

APDHB et al (2004) *Para que no se olvide*. 12–13 de febrero de 2003, Plural, La Paz.

Archondo, Rafael (1991) *Compadres al micrófono. La resurrección metropolitana del ayllu*, HISBOL, La Paz.

Arnold, Denise (coord.) (1998) *Hacia un orden andino de las cosas*, Hisbol La Paz.

Arnold, Denise y Spedding, Alison (2005) *Mujeres en los movimientos sociales en Bolivia, 2000–2003*, Cidem, La Paz.

Barrera, Augusto (2001) *Acción colectiva y crisis política. El movimiento indígena ecuatoriano en la década de los noventa*, Osal/Abya Yala, Quito.

Bretón Solo de Zaldívar, Víctor (2001) "Capital social, etnicidad y desarrollo: algunas consideraciones críticas desde los Andes ecuatorianos," revista *Yachaikuna* No. 2, December, Instituto Científico de Culturas Indígenas, Quito.

Calderón, Fernando y Szmukler, Alicia (2000) *La política en las calles*, Ceres/Uasb/Plural, La Paz.

Capra, Fritjof (1998) *La trama de la vida*, Barcelona, Anagrama.

Castillo Collado, Martín (2005) *Aprendiendo con el corazón. El tejido andino en la educación quechua*, Pinseib, Proeib, Plural, La Paz.

CEDLA (1999) *Diagnóstico socioeconómico de El Alto. Distritos 5 y 6*, La Paz.

———. (2000) *Ser productor en El Alto*, Cedla, La Paz.

Choque, María Eugenia y Mamani, Carlos (2003) "Reconstitución del Ayllu y derechos de los Pueblos Indígenas: El Movimiento Indio en los Andes de Bolivia", en *Ticona, Esteban, Los Andes desde los Andes*.

Choque, Vidal (2005) *Desde el fondo de nosotros mismos*, Indymedia, La Paz.

CIPCA (1992) "Futuro de la comunidad campesina," *Cuaderno de Investigación* No. 35, La Paz.

Clastres, Pierre (1978) *La sociedad contra el Estado*, Monte Avila, Caracas.

———. (1981) *Investigaciones en antropología política*, Gedisa, Barcelona.

———. (2001) *Crónica de los indios guayaquís*, Alta Fulla, Barcelona.

———. (2004) *Arqueología de la violencia: la guerra en las sociedades primitivas*, FCE, Buenos Aires.

Colectivo Situaciones.(2005) *Mal de altura*, Tinta Limón, Buenos Aires.

Condo Riveros Freddy (1996) *Las Bartolinas. Sus orígenes, su historia y su futuro*, FNMCB-BS, La Paz.

Confederación de Nacionalidades Indígenas de Ecuador-CONAIE (1990) *Las nacionalidades indígenas en el Ecuador*, Tincui/Abya Yala, Quito.

———. (2001) *Proyecto Político*, Quito, www.conaie.org

Contreras Baspineiro, Alex (1994) *La marcha histórica*, Cedib, Cochabamba.

Dávalos, Pablo (2000) "Ecuador: las transformaciones políticas del movimiento indígena ecuatoriano", OSAL No. 1, Clacso, Buenos Aires, June 2000.

———. (2001) "Movimiento indígena ecuatoriano: la constitución de un actor político," *Cuestiones de América* No. 7, November, www.cuestiones.ws

———. (2004) "Movimiento indígena, Estado y plurinacionalidad en Ecuador", Revista Venezolana de Economía y Ciencias Sociales vol. 10 No. 1, (January–April), Caracas, pp. 175–202.

Dávalos Pablo (ed. (2005) *Pueblos indígenas, Estado y democracia*, Clacso, Buenos Aires.

Decreto Reglamentario a la ley de Participación Popular y Descentralización, No. 24.447, December 20, 1996, Presidencia de Bolivia, La Paz.

Deleuze, Gilles (2005) *La isla desierta y otros textos*, Pre-Textos, Valencia.

———. (2003) *En medio de Spinoza*, Cactus, Buenos Aires.

———. (1994) *Mil mesetas*, Pre-Textos, Valencia.

Delgado Mancilla, Abraham (2005a) *De las elecciones a la insurrección...¡Carajo!*, Amuyawi, El Alto.

———. (2005b) *Rebelión de mayo-junio*. Cronología, s/e, El Alto.

Díaz-Polanco, Héctor (1996) *Autonomía regional*, Siglo XXI, México.

———. (1997) *La rebelión zapatista y la autonomía*, Siglo XXI, México.

———. (2005) "Etnofagia y multiculturalismo," *Memoria periodical* No. 200, October, México.

Díaz-Polanco, Héctor y Sánchez, Consuelo (2002) *México diverso. El debate por la autonomía*, Siglo XXI, México.

Diócesis de El Alto (2004) *Memoria testimonial de la guerra del gas*, Cáritas/Comisión de Hermandad/Diócesis de El Alto, El Alto.

Dunkerley, James (1987) *Rebelión en las venas*, Quipus, La Paz.

Ecuarunari (1989) "Taller Andino de Intercambio de Experiencias en Educación y Comunicación de Organizaciones Campesino-Indígenas," Ecuarunari, Quito.

Erbol (1995) "Estrategia de comunicación alternativa para el desarrollo," La Paz.

Escárzaga, Fabiola y Gutiérrez, Raquel (coords.) (2005) *Movimiento indígena en América Latina: resistencia y proyecto alternativo*, Benemérita Universidad Autónoma de Puebla, México.

FEJUVE-El Alto (2003) *Estatuto Orgánico*, Federación de Juntas Vecinales FEJUVE-El Alto.

Fernández, Marcelo (2004) *La ley del ayllu*, Pieb, La Paz.

Flores Gonzáles, Elba (2005) "La justicia comunitaria un verdadero sistema, in *Justicia Comunitaria*, Poder Judicial, Sucre.

Foucault, Michael (1996) *Historia de la sexualidad, tomo I* "La voluntad de saber," Siglo XXI, México.

García Linera, Alvaro (1999) *Reproletarización. Nueva clase obrera y desarrollo del capital industrial en Bolivia (1952–1998)*, Muela del Diablo, La Paz.

———. (2001) *La condición obrera*, Muela del Diablo/Idis-Umsa, La Paz.

———. (coord.) (2004a) *Sociología de los movimientos sociales en Bolivia*, Diakonia-Oxfam, La Paz.

———. (2004b) "La crisis del Estado y las sublevaciones indígeno-plebeyas", in *Memorias de octubre*, Luis Tapia, Raúl Prada, Alvaro García Linera, Comuna, La Paz.

———. (2004c) "Democracia liberal vs. democracia comunitaria", *El Juguete Rabioso*, January 20, 2004, La Paz.

———. (2005) *Estado multinacional. Una propuesta democrática y pluralista para la extinción de la exclusión de las naciones indias*, Malatesta, La Paz.

García, Alvaro et al (2000) *El retorno de la Bolivia plebeya*, Muela del Diablo, La Paz.

———. (2001a) *Pluriverso. Teoría política boliviana*, Muela del Diablo, La Paz.

———. (2001b) *Tiempos de rebelión*, Muela del Diablo, La Paz.

Gilly, Adolfo (2003) "Historia desde adentro" en Forrest Hylton et al *Ya es otro tiempo el presente. Cuatro momentos de insurgencia indígena*, Muela del Diablo, La Paz.

Gómez, Luis A.(2004) *El Alto de pie. Una insurrección aymara en Bolivia*, Comuna-Indymedia-HDP, La Paz.

Guaygua, Germán et al (2000) *Ser joven en El Alto. Rupturas y continuidades en la tradición cultural*, Pieb, La Paz.

Guha, Ranahit (2002) *Las voces de la historia*, Crítica, Madrid.

Guerin, Daniel (2003), *Rosa Luxemburgo o la espontaneidad revolucionaria*, Anarres, Buenos Aires.

Guerrero Cazar, Fernando y Ospina Peralta, Pablo (2003) *El poder de la comunidad*, Clacso, Buenos Aires.

Gutiérrez, Raquel (1999) *Desandar el laberinto*, Muela del Diablo, La Paz.

———. (2001) *Forma comunal y liberal de la política*, Comuna, La Paz.

Gutiérrez, Raquel et al (2002) *Democratizaciones plebeyas*, Muela del Diablo, La Paz.

Harris, Olivia (1987) *Economía étnica*, Hisbol, La Paz.

Harris, Olivia y Albó, Xavier (1986) *Monteras y guardatojos*, Cipca, La Paz.

Hobsbawm, Eric (1995) *Historia del siglo XX*, Crítica, Barcelona.

Holloway, John (2002) *Cambiar el mundo sin tomar el poder*, Herramienta, Buenos Aires.

Hurtado, Javier (1986) *El Katarismo*, Hisbol, La Paz.

Indaburu Quintana, Rafael (2004) *Evaluación de la ciudad de El Alto*, en www.usaidbolivia.org.bo/StudiesAndReports/InformeFinal-ElAlto.pdf

Instituto Científico de Culturas Indígenas (ICCI) (2005) Boletín Ary Rimay, "Los dilemas de la CONAIE" ICCI, *Quito*, No. 70, January, in http//:icci.nativeweb.org

Kusch, Rodolfo (1977) *El pensamiento indígena y popular en América*, Hachette, Buenos Aires.

Lenin, V. I. (1976) *¿Qué hacer?*, *Obras Completas*, Tomo V, Madrid, Akal.

Lenkersdorf, Carlos (2004) *Conceptos tojolabales de filosofía y del altermundismo*, Plaza y Valdés, México.

Ley de Municipalidades No. 2028 del 28 de octubre de 1999, Congreso Nacional de Bolivia, La Paz.

Ley de Participación Popular No. 1551, April 20, 1993, Congreso Nacional de Bolivia, La Paz.

Lewin, Boleslao (1973) *Tupac Amaru*, Siglo Veinte, Buenos Aires.

Lima Chavez, Constantino (2003) *Wiphala del Tahuantinsuyu*, pamphlet, La Paz.

Lossovsky, Drizdo (1930) *De la huelga a la toma del poder. Los combates económicos y nuestra táctica*, Montevideo, Conferencia Sindical Latinoamericana.

Lucas, Kintto (2000) *La rebelión de los indios*, Abya Yala, Quito.

Mamani Ramírez, Pablo (2004a) *El rugir de las multitudes*, Yachaywasi, La Paz.

——. (2004b) *Microgobiernos barriales en el levantamiento de la ciudad de El Alto*, El Alto, unpublished.

——. (2004c) *Universidad y Multiversidad*, El Alto, unpublished.

——. (2005) *Geopolíticas indígenas*, CADES, El Alto.

Mansilla, H. C. F. (2005) *Para entender la Constitución Política del Estado*, Corte Nacional Electoral, La Paz.

Marx, Karl y Engels, Federico (1980) *El porvenir de la comuna rural rusa*, Cuadernos de Pasado y Presente 90, México.

Marx, Karl (1980) *La guerra civil en Francia*, Editorial Progreso, Moscú.

Maturana, Alberto y Varela, Francisco (1996) *El árbol del conocimiento*, Madrid, Debate.

——. (1995) *De máquinas y seres vivos*, editorial Universitaria, Santiago.

Mier Cueto, Enrique (2005) "Las prácticas jurídicas aymaras desde una perspectiva cultural", in *Justicia Comunitaria*, Poder Judicial, Sucre.

Movimiento Katarista de Liberación (1990) *Modelo social del ayllu. Pensamiento katarista*, MKL, La Paz.

Mujeres Creando (s/f) *Porque la memoria no es puro cuento*, Mujeres Creando, La Paz.

Mujeres Creando y Colectivo Situaciones (2005) *La virgen de los deseos*, Tinta Limón, Buenos Aires.

Murra, John (1975) *Formaciones económicas y políticas del mundo andino*, IEP, Lima.

Negri, Antonio (2003) *Spinoza subversivo*, Akal, Madrid.

——. (2003) *Job, la fuerza del esclavo*, Paidós, Buenos Aires.

——. (2003) *La forma-Estado*, Akal, Madrid.

Negri, Antonio y Hardt, Michael (2003) *El trabajo de Dionisos*, Akal, Madrid.

O'Phelan Godoy, Scarlett (1985) *Un siglo de rebeliones anticoloniales. Perú y Bolivia. 1700–1783*, Centro de Estudios Rurales Andinos Bartolomé de las Casas, Cusco.

Pashukanis, Evgeni (1976) *Teoría general del derecho y marxismo*, Labor, Barcelona.

Patzi Paco, Félix (1996) *Economía comunera y explotación capitalista*, Edcom, La Paz.

———. (1999) *Insurgencia y sumisión. Movimientos indígeno-campesinos (1983–1998)*, Comuna, La Paz.

———. (2001) *Etnofagia estatal. Modernas formas de violencia simbólica*, Instituto de Investigaciones Sociológicas, La Paz.

———. (2003a) "Todo lo que caduca merece perecer", en *Memoria testimonial de la guerra del gas*, Cáritas-Diocesis, El Alto.

———. (2003b) "Rebelión indígena contra la colonialidad y la transnacionalización de la economía: triunfos y vicisitudes del movimiento indígena desde 2000 a 2003", en Forrest Hylton et al *Ya es otro tiempo el presente. Cuatro momentos de insurgencia indígena*, Muela del Diablo, La Paz.

———. (2004) *Sistema comunal. Una propuesta alternativa al sistema liberal*, CEA, La Paz.

Poder Judicial (2005) *Justicia comunitaria en los pueblos originarios de Bolivia*, Instituto de la Judicatura de Bolivia, Sucre.

Porto Gonçalvez, Carlos Walter (2001) *Geo-grafías. Movimientos sociales, nuevas territorialidades y sustentabilidad*, Siglo XXI, México.

Prada, Raúl (2004) *Largo octubre*, Plural, La Paz.

Prigogine, Ilya y Stengers, Isabelle (1990) *La nueva alianza, Metamorfosis de la ciencia*, Alianza, Madrid.

Proyecto de Apoyo a la Reforma Educativa (PAR) (2005) *El Alto: nueve aspectos que configuran la ciudad*, PAR, El Alto.

Quisbert Quispe, Máximo (2003) *FEJUVE El Alto 1990–1998. Dilemas del clientelismo colectivo en un mercado político en expansión*, Aruwiyiri, La Paz.

Qhispi Wanka, Felipe (1990) *Tupak Katari vive y vuelve…carajo*, Ofensiva Roja, La Paz.

Quispe, Felipe (2005) "La lucha de los ayllus kataristas hoy", in *Movimiento indígena en América Latina: resistencia y proyecto alternativo*, Benemérita Universidad Autónoma de Puebla, México.

Quispe, Marco (2004) *De ch'usa marka a jach'a marka*, Plural-Wayna Tambo, El Alto.

Ramón Valarezo, Galo (1993) *El regreso de los runas*, Comunidec, Quito.

Reinaga, Fausto (1953) *Tierra y libertad. La revolución nacional y el indio*, Rumbo Sindical, La Paz.

———. (1981) *La revolución amáutica*, CAM, La Paz.

———. (2001) *La revolución india*, Fundación Amáutica Fausto Reinaga, La Paz.

———. (2003) *Tesis India*, Hilda Reinaga, La Paz.

Regalsky, Pablo (2003) *Etnicidad y clase. El Estado boliviano y las estrategias andinas de manejo de su espacio*, Ceidis/Cesu-Umss/Cenda/Plural, La Paz.

Rivera Cusicanqui, Silvia (1983) "Luchas campesinas contemporáneas en Bolivia: el movimiento 'katarista': 1970–1980" in René Zavaleta Mercado (ed.) *Bolivia hoy*, Siglo XXI, México.

———. (1990) "El potencial epistemológico y teórico de la historia oral: de la lógica instrumental a la descolonización de la historia," in *Temas Sociales*, La Paz, No. 11.

———. (1991) *Pachakuti: los aymara de Bolivia frente a medio milenio de colonialismo*, THOA, La Paz.

———. (2003) *Oprimidos pero no vencidos*, Aruwiyiri-Yachaywasi, La Paz.

———. (2004) "Metáforas y retóricas en el levantamiento de octubre", in *Bolivian Studies Journal/Revista*, Vol 4, Issue 1.

———. (s/f) *Bircholas*, Mama Huaco, La Paz.

Rivera Cusicanqui, Silvia y Barragán, Rossana (ed.) (1997) *Debates post coloniales. Una introducción a los estudios de la subalternidad*, Sephis/Aruwiyiri, La Paz.

Rovira, Guiomar (1997) *Mujeres de maíz*, Era, México.

Sandóval, Godofredo y Sostres, Fernanda (1989) *La ciudad prometida*, Ildis, La Paz.

Sandóval, Godofredo et al (1987) *Chukiyawu. La cara aymara de La Paz. IV. Nuevos lazos con el campo*, CIPCA, La Paz.

Sarango, Luis Fernando (2004) "La administración de justicia indígena en Ecuador," *Yachaikuna*, Quito, julio.

Skocpol, Theda (1984) *Los Estados y las revoluciones sociales*, FCE, México.

Scott, James (2000) *Los dominados y el arte de la resistencia*, ERA, México.

Spedding, Alison (2003) *Breve curso de parentesco*, Mamahuaco, La Paz.

Stefanoni, Pablo (2004) "Algunas reflexiones sobre el MAS-IPSP," en *Temas Sociales* No. 25, Idis, La Paz.

Subcomandante Insurgente Marcos (2004) "La velocidad del sueño (III): Pies desnudos," *Rebeldía* No. 24, México, October.

Tapia, Luis (2002) *La condición multisocietal*, Muela del Diablo, La Paz.

———. (2002) *La velocidad del pluralismo*, Muela del diablo, La Paz.

Ticona Alejo, Esteban (2005) "La rebelión aymara y popular de octubre de 2003", en Pablo Dávalos (comp.) *Pueblos indígenas, Estado y democracia*, Clacso, Buenos Aires.

Tapia, Luis et al *Memorias de octubre*, Muela del diablo, La Paz.

Ticona Alejo, Esteban (1997) *La lucha por el poder comunal. Jesús de Machaqa, la marka rebelde*, vol. 3, Cedoin-Cipca, La Paz.

Ticona Alejo, Esteban (ed.) (2003) *Los Andes desde los Andes*, Yachaywasi, La Paz.

Wallerstein, Immanuel (1998) "Marx y el subdesarrollo", in *Impensar las ciencias sociales*, Siglo XXI, México.

Weber, Max (2002) *Economía y sociedad*, FCE, Madrid.

Zavaleta Mercado, René (ed.) (1983) *Bolivia hoy*, Siglo XXI, México.

Zavaleta Mercado, René (1987) *El poder dual*, Los Amigos del Libro, Cochabamba.

——. (1992) *50 años de historia*, Los Amigos del Libro, Cochabamba.

Zibechi, Raúl (1995) *Los arroyos cuando bajan. Los desafíos del zapatismo*, Nordan, Montevideo.

——. (1997) *La revuelta juvenil de los 90*, Nordan, Montevideo.

——. (1999) *La mirada horizontal. Movimientos sociales y emancipación*, Nordan, Montevideo.

——. (2003) *Genealogía de la revuelta*, Letra Libre, Buenos Aires.

——. (2005a) *La emancipación como producción de vínculos*, Clacso, Buenos Aires.

——. (2005b) "Subterranean Echos: Resistance and Politics 'desde el sótano,'" *Socialism and Democracy*, vol. 19 No. 3 Routledge, Oxfordshire, November.

——. (2005c) "Espacios, territorios y regiones: la creatividad social de los nuevos movimientos en América Latina," *Contrahistorias* No. 5, México, September.

Magazines, periodicals and other sources

Agencia de Prensa Alteña, daily dispatches 2004–2005.

El Juguete Rabioso, periódico semanal, La Paz, 2000–2005.

Indymedia, "Aunque se caiga el cielo. La lucha de los movimientos sociales en Bolivia," La Paz, 2004.

Le Monde Diplomatique, edición Bolivia, 2003–2005.

Pulso, semanario, La Paz, 2003–2005.

Radio Erbol, "Jornadas de octubre 2003," transmisiones de Radio Erbol, 100.9.

Interviews

Alvaro García Linera, sociólogo, Niteroi (Brazil), October 15, 2005.

Abraham Delgado, Jóvenes de Octubre, La Paz, July 26, 2005.

Oscar Olivera, leader of the Coordinadora del Agua, Cochabamba July 2005 and Montevideo, October 27, 2005.

Pablo Mamani Ramírez, sociologist, director of the Sociología de la Universidad Pública de El Alto (UPEA), El Alto, July 22, 2005.

Bruno Rojas, CEDLA, La Paz, July 27, 2005.

Juan Carlos Condori, Achacachi, July 23, 2005.

Silvia Rivera Cusicanqui, antropóloga, La Paz, July 19/20, 2005.

Félix Patzi Paco, sociólogo La Paz, July 19, 2005.

Colectiva a Jóvenes de Octubre (Abraham, Elías Uvaldo, Alex y Jhony), El Alto, July 18, 2005.

Marco Quispe, El Alto, July 25, 2005.

Julio Mamani Conde, director of Agencia Popular El Alto (APA), El Alto, July 25, 2005.

Abraham Grandidier, of the Asociación de los Sistemas Comunitarios de Agua (Asica Sur), Cochabamba, July 30, 2005.

Mujeres Creando, La Paz, July, 2005.

Index

ADN. *See* Alianza Democrática Nacionalista (ADN)

Achacachi, Bolivia, 59

Achacachi Manifesto, 101, 104–5, 107

Aché people. *See* Guayaqui people

Adrián, Rosario, 92, 93

adultery: punishment for, 99

Alianza Democrática Nacionalista (ADN), 77. *See also* Patriotic Agreement (ADN-MIR)

Amaru, Tupac, 130

Andean culture, 19, 25, 57, 73, 109n29, 113; CONDEPA and, 73–74

aptapis, 52, 58

Archondo, Rafael, 24–25

Argentina, 7. *See also* Buenos Aires

armed struggle. *See* war

armies. *See* Aymara people: army of; Bolivian army

Ary Rimay Bulletin, 124

assemblies. *See* mass assemblies; sovereign assemblies

assimilation, 128

authoritarianism, 16

autonomous regional government, 115, 116, 121

autonomy, 89, 112, 122, 137–39 passim; of indigenous people, 118, 121–22, 131–33 passim; in labor management, 39; municipal, 34, 73; of representatives, 88; workplace, 39

ayllus, 2, 15, 20, 26, 104–13 passim,

132; law and, 97; militarized, 51, 54–55; subdivision of, 19n29; urban resurrection of, 25, 74

Aymara people, 2n1, 7, 12, 37; army of, 54–55, 120; communications and, 58–62; community justice and, 91–99; decision making and, 47; family business and, 40–41; leadership and, 46; neighborhood councils and, 26; organization of society, 53n34; rural–urban migration of, 17–24 passim; state and, 56, 67, 88, 101–33 passim. *See also* El Alto, Bolivia

Aymara women, 74–75

ayni. See mutual aid

Banzer, Hugo, 77

barracks (social relations), 53–55 passim. *See also* Qalachaka barracks

barricades, 13, 48, 51–52, 62

barrios, 30, 35, 53, 56, 67, 69

bicycles, 52

blockades, 12, 13, 16, 49–54 passim, 105, 109, 110. *See also* barricades

Bolivian army, 43, 50, 54, 84, 106; invasion of Achacachi, 105

Bolivian revolution (1952). *See* revolution and revolutions: Bolivia (1952)

bourgeoisie, 2, 18

Brazil, 2

Breton, Victor, 129

Buenos Aires, 89n64

"Passim" (literally "scattered") indicates intermittent discussion of a topic over a cluster of pages.

water, 23; community administration
    of, 16, 25, 27, 28, 79, 119, 140
"water wars," 2, 6, 105, 113
Weber, Max, 15, 29, 87
What Is to Be Done? (Lenin), 45, 47
whipping of adulterers, 99
whistles, 61, 62, 91, 93
women, 112; division of labor and,
    48; jailbreaks engineered by,
    75; leadership by, 40, 68, 75; in
    neighborhood councils, 26; Zap-
    atista, 122
women television hosts, 74–75
women workers: El Alto, 37, 39
work rotation. *See* labor rotation
worker autonomy, 39
World Bank, 126–27, 130

youth, 81, 112

Zapatistas, xiii, xiv, 1, 6, 7, 99, 121–
    22, 130–31
Zasúlich, Vera, 117

Support AK Press!

AK Press is one of the world's largest and most productive

anarchist publishing houses. We're entirely worker-run and democratically managed. We operate without a corporate structure—no boss, no managers, no bullshit. We publish close to twenty books every year, and distribute thousands of other titles published by other like-minded independent presses from around the globe.

The Friends of AK program is a way that you can directly contribute to the continued existence of AK Press, and ensure that we're able to keep publishing great books just like this one! Friends pay a minimum of $25 per month, for a minimum three month period, into our publishing account. In return, Friends automatically receive (for the duration of their membership), as they appear, one free copy of every new AK Press title. They're also entitled to a 20% discount on everything featured in the AK Press Distribution catalog and on the website, on any and every order. You or your organization can even sponsor an entire book if you should so choose!

There's great stuff in the works—so sign up now to become a Friend of AK Press, and let the presses roll!

Won't you be our friend? Email friendsofak@akpress.org for more info, or visit the Friends of AK Press website: http://www.akpress.org/programs/friendsofak